I0410786

ACCOUNTABILITY, POLICIES, AND TACTICS OF LAW ENFORCEMENT WITHIN THE DEPARTMENT OF THE INTERIOR AND THE U.S. FOREST SERVICE

OVERSIGHT HEARING

BEFORE THE

SUBCOMMITTEE ON OVERSIGHT AND INVESTIGATIONS

OF THE

COMMITTEE ON NATURAL RESOURCES U.S. HOUSE OF REPRESENTATIVES

ONE HUNDRED FOURTEENTH CONGRESS

FIRST SESSION

Tuesday, July 28, 2015

Serial No. 114–17

Printed for the use of the Committee on Natural Resources

Available via the World Wide Web: http://www.fdsys.gov
or
Committee address: http://naturalresources.house.gov

U.S. GOVERNMENT PUBLISHING OFFICE

95–713 PDF   WASHINGTON : 2016

For sale by the Superintendent of Documents, U.S. Government Publishing Office
Internet: bookstore.gpo.gov   Phone: toll free (866) 512–1800; DC area (202) 512–1800
Fax: (202) 512–2104   Mail: Stop IDCC, Washington, DC 20402–0001

COMMITTEE ON NATURAL RESOURCES

ROB BISHOP, UT, *Chairman*
RAÚL M. GRIJALVA, AZ, *Ranking Democratic Member*

Don Young, AK
Louie Gohmert, TX
Doug Lamborn, CO
Robert J. Wittman, VA
John Fleming, LA
Tom McClintock, CA
Glenn Thompson, PA
Cynthia M. Lummis, WY
Dan Benishek, MI
Jeff Duncan, SC
Paul A. Gosar, AZ
Raúl R. Labrador, ID
Doug LaMalfa, CA
Jeff Denham, CA
Paul Cook, CA
Bruce Westerman, AR
Garret Graves, LA
Dan Newhouse, WA
Ryan K. Zinke, MT
Jody B. Hice, GA
Aumua Amata Coleman Radewagen, AS
Thomas MacArthur, NJ
Alexander X. Mooney, WV
Cresent Hardy, NV
Vacancy

Grace F. Napolitano, CA
Madeleine Z. Bordallo, GU
Jim Costa, CA
Gregorio Kilili Camacho Sablan, CNMI
Niki Tsongas, MA
Pedro R. Pierluisi, PR
Jared Huffman, CA
Raul Ruiz, CA
Alan S. Lowenthal, CA
Matt Cartwright, PA
Donald S. Beyer, Jr., VA
Norma J. Torres, CA
Debbie Dingell, MI
Ruben Gallego, AZ
Lois Capps, CA
Jared Polis, CO
Wm. Lacy Clay, MO

Jason Knox, *Chief of Staff*
Lisa Pittman, *Chief Counsel*
David Watkins, *Democratic Staff Director*
Sarah Parker, *Democratic Deputy Chief Counsel*

———

SUBCOMMITTEE ON OVERSIGHT AND INVESTIGATIONS

LOUIE GOHMERT, TX, *Chairman*
DEBBIE DINGELL, MI, *Ranking Democratic Member*

Doug Lamborn, CO
Raúl R. Labrador, ID
Bruce Westerman, AR
Jody B. Hice, GA
Aumua Amata Coleman Radewagen, AS
Alexander X. Mooney, WV
Vacancy
Rob Bishop, UT, *ex officio*

Jared Huffman, CA
Ruben Gallego, AZ
Jared Polis, CO
Wm. Lacy Clay, MO
Vacancy
Raúl M. Grijalva, AZ, *ex officio*

———

CONTENTS

OVERSIGHT HEARING ON ACCOUNTABILITY, POLICIES, AND TACTICS OF LAW ENFORCEMENT WITHIN THE DEPARTMENT OF THE INTERIOR AND THE U.S. FOREST SERVICE

Tuesday, July 28, 2015

U.S. House of Representatives

Subcommittee on Oversight and Investigations

Committee on Natural Resources

Washington, DC

The subcommittee met, pursuant to notice, at 10:30 a.m., in room 1324, Longworth House Office Building, Hon. Louie Gohmert, [Chairman of the Subcommittee] presiding.

Present: Representatives Gohmert, Westerman, Hice, Radewagen, Mooney, Bishop (ex officio); Dingell, Huffman, and Gallego.

Mr. GOHMERT. The Subcommittee on Oversight and Investigations will come to order.

This subcommittee is meeting today to hear testimony on accountability, policies, and tactics of law enforcement within the Department of the Interior and the U.S. Forest Service.

Under Committee Rule 4(f), any oral statements at this hearing are limited to the Chairman and Ranking Minority Member. This will allow us to hear from our witnesses sooner and let Members keep to their schedules.

Therefore, I ask unanimous consent that all other Members' opening statements for this meeting be made part of the hearing record if they are submitted to the Subcommittee Clerk by 5:00 p.m. today.

Hearing no objection, so ordered.

Also, I politely ask that everyone in this hearing please silence your cell phones. Make sure that there is nothing that goes off. When I was a judge, I would have my bailiff confiscate any phones that went off; and then you had to do a couple hundred hours of community service to get it back. I do not have a bailiff here as such; so I just have to ask that you keep your cell phone silent, please. Thank you.

All right. I will now recognize myself for 5 minutes for an opening statement.

STATEMENT OF THE HON. LOUIE GOHMERT, A REPRESENTATIVE IN CONGRESS FROM THE STATE OF TEXAS

Mr. GOHMERT. Today we are discussing the accountability of law enforcement within our land management agencies. I would like to recognize from the start the important work of hundreds of law enforcement employees from the Department of the Interior to the U.S. Forest Service. These men and women risk everything to protect our iconic landmarks, natural resources, as well as critical energy infrastructure.

Just last year, 38-year-old Forest Service Officer Jason Crisp and his K-9 partner were killed while pursuing an armed murder suspect. That was a horrible tragedy, and his sacrifice should be remembered by all of us.

Clearly, there are many, many excellent officers out there just doing their job day in and day out. Unfortunately, we have come to learn of situations that place local law enforcement officers at odds with their Federal counterparts.

I would like to enter into the record an article from the *Salt Lake Tribune* published in October of 2014, entitled "Utah to BLM: Rein in Your Cops."

The article begins, "Public Enemy No. 1 for rural Utah sheriffs just happens to be a fellow peace officer named Dan Love, the Bureau of Land Management's special agent in charge."

[The article submitted for the record by Mr. Gohmert follows:]

Utah to BLM: Rein in your cops

By Brian Maffly
The Salt Lake Tribune
Published October 19, 2014 10:12 am

Law enforcement • Sheriffs say federal rangers overstep their authority and blame Utah-Nevada special agent for escalation of conflicts.

Public Enemy No. 1 for rural Utah sheriffs just happens to be a fellow peace officer: Dan Love, the Bureau of Land Management's special agent in charge.

Elected law enforcement officers from Nephi to Blanding call him an arrogant and dishonest bully who has little regard for local authority and dodges accountability, derailing a collaborative approach to police work on the state's federal lands.

Love reportedly just laughed when Garfield County Sheriff James "Danny" Perkins relayed ranchers' complaints about federal officers removing plastic feed tubs from the range and threatening the ranchers with litter citations.

He drew early controversy during an undercover probe of artifacts trafficking in Blanding in 2009. More recently, Love led the BLM's aborted roundup of Cliven Bundy's cattle following an armed standoff with anti-government protesters at the Utah-Nevada border.

While tensions with federal authority are hardly new to Utah, local officials say friction has intensified with Love at the helm of BLM law enforcement in Utah and Nevada.

Now top state officials want Love gone. "This is untenable," said Lt. Gov. Spencer Cox. "There comes a time when personalities get in the way of productivity."

For his part, Love is not talking.

Local officials may share some of the blame for the poor relations. According to court filings, elected leaders and even deputies have confronted BLM rangers, publicly challenging their authority.

But Love's critics say his intimidating attitude and unwillingness to consult with counties exemplify a "culture of arrogance" that undermines cooperation in Utah's remote reaches. The public loses, safety is compromised and tax dollars are wasted, Utah's rural sheriffs say.

"This refusal to coordinate, coupled with a lack of any meaningful oversight, has created a perfect environment where the abuse of federal law enforcement powers can occur," Perkins recently testified before a congressional committee.

For example, Perkins and San Juan County Sheriff Rick Eldredge say, rangers pull over citizens without probable cause, even in areas where they have no jurisdiction, "bully" ranch hands, berate tourists for parking vehicles off dirt roads and illegally close roads. Federal officers refuse to help with searches and rescues, or when they do, they get in the way.

BLM law enforcement officials would not speak on the record, but an agency spokeswoman said BLM does takes complaints seriously.

"When we receive specifics regarding these allegations, we look into the incidents and take corrective action if appropriate," Celia Boddington said. "However, it is difficult for us to address allegations when they are either not reported to us or reported several months after the event."

Still, the agency is revising its command structure to make law enforcement responsive to local concerns.

"We enjoy positive and constructive relations with the majority of sheriffs," Boddington said, "and couldn't get our job done without working closely with them and their teams."

———

Broken accords • One recent flap surrounding Love stems from the contracts the BLM signs with some sheriff's departments, compensating them for patrolling public lands and conducting searches and rescues.

State and local officials allege Love recently "terminated" such contracts with five counties as retribution for the state's enactment last year of HB155, which limits the authority of officers employed by federal land agencies.

While discussing the contracts with BLM's top law enforcement official, Salvatore Lauro, recently, Cox asked him to assign a new special agent in charge for Utah.

"They are not willing to make that replacement at this time," Cox said, "but they are willing to work toward improving those relations."

The lieutenant governor said he and other state officials have negotiated face to face with Love, and have gotten nowhere.

"If I was going to battle, I'd want him beside me," Cox told a recent meeting of Utah's Commission on Federalism. "But I don't want him instigating a war."

Love has declined lawmakers' invitation to speak at legislative committees. BLM officials won't discuss individual employees and wouldn't make Love available for an interview.

But they denied retribution played any role in the contract decisions.

According to Boddington, the BLM allowed the contracts to expire after higher-ups found them legally defective during routine reviews. Agreements with Kane, San Juan, Emery, Juab and Grand county sheriffs—worth about $178,000 a year—expired in 2012.

"The BLM's review of the contracts was underway prior to the bill introduction," she said. "There is no connection of any kind between our review and HB155."

To patrol Utah's 23 million acres of public lands, the BLM employs 15 uniformed rangers or field officers. Seven special agents who investigate violations of federal law related to public lands and natural resources also work for BLM, which administers about 40 percent of Utah's land base. All report in varying degrees to Love, who has served in the top spot for less than a decade.

———

Threat to public safety? • The situation has become so tense, or perhaps juvenile, that federal and local officers sometimes threaten to arrest each other.

Garfield and at least three other counties have passed resolutions declaring federal authority unwelcome, alleging BLM law enforcement presents a threat to "health, safety and welfare."

Retired rangers say the tensions date back to the 1970s, when the BLM began assigning field rangers. Controversial BLM operations, such as the artifact raids in Blanding or the Bundy standoff at Bunkerville, Nev., bring "long-simmering" resentments to the surface, said Ed Patrovsky, who patrolled the 3.2-million-acre Craig district spanning parts of nine northwest Colorado counties.

"The problems lie on both sides," Patrovsky said. "Some sheriffs are territorial. They see federal officers as competitors rather than cooperators. Some of the federal officers come in with the same attitude."

He said the BLM's hiring patterns in the past two decades have contributed to the problem. Instead of recruiting rangers from other land agencies, it now tends to tap agencies such as the Border Patrol and Bureau of Prisons.

"They are hiring rangers that don't have the natural resource ethic that ties them to the land," Patrovsky said.

Still, today's widespread anti-federal sentiment complicates rangers' jobs.

"Things can snowball and gather their own momentum without any fault on the part of the ranger," said Patrovsky, who was deputized by the Moffat County sheriff during his years in Craig. "There is an atmosphere of fear and intimidation out there and rangers are afraid to speak out."

It is common for Utah sheriffs to deputize U.S. Forest Service and National Park Service officers, but no BLM rangers are currently deputized in Utah.

———

'He had no jurisdiction' • BLM arrest statistics seem to undermine claims of an overbearing presence. Rangers made just three arrests in Utah in 2012, and issued 27 citations and 110 warnings.

County officials, however, say they are more concerned with incidents that don't wind up in court, but illustrate a lack of respect toward the sheriff's role as a county's chief law enforcement officer. At a recent congressional hearing, Garfield County Commissioner Leland Pollock likened BLM law enforcement operations to "the Gestapo."

Perkins said tourists have complained they will never return to Garfield County after their treatment by rangers in the Grand Staircase Escalante National Monument.

In his legislative testimony, Eldredge said a BLM ranger confronted him on his family's property adjacent to BLM land and the Ute Mountain Ute community. The ranger, who didn't recognize the sheriff, erroneously admonished Eldredge against driving on tribal land. The ranger backed off and apologized when Eldredge identified himself, but the sheriff was in no forgiving mood.

"He didn't even know whose land it was," Eldredge told lawmakers earlier this month. "He just wanted to give me a bad time. Even if it was [land administered by Bureau of Indian Affairs], he had no jurisdiction to tell me stay off."

Many county leaders don't hesitate to praise BLM Utah Director Juan Palma, regarded as a warm public servant committed to bridging the federal-state divide.

But whatever goodwill Palma builds, Love and officers under his command put a match to it, local officials say.

Pollock points to an effort by Garfield County officials to hammer out a law enforcement contract with the BLM, similar to the agency's agreement with neighboring Kane County. Garfield County is also home to the Grand Staircase monument, and last year, its six-deputy department spent $70,000 on helicopter time and 265 staff hours rescuing monument visitors.

Love refused to execute a contract, according to Pollock.

"We budgeted based on my negotiations with Juan Palma, and all of the sudden he said he couldn't do it," Pollock said. "That's sick and wrong. We hired a deputy that would have made the Grand Staircase a safer place, and this one guy killed it."

Meanwhile, Perkins contends the BLM ranger assigned to the county refuses to coordinate with deputies on searches and rescues. He once prematurely called in a helicopter, Perkins said, which sat idle for four hours before it returned to base, refueled, and came back with another pilot.

———

BLM cops and civilians • Counties also complain that BLM law enforcement operates at cross purposes with its own civilian land-management staff.

Perkins and Pollock cited an incident where a ranger posted roads with closed signs shortly before the opening of a limited entry hunt. Locals complained to the BLM field manager, who determined that the roads should be open, according to the sheriff.

But when the manager took down the signs, the BLM ranger threatened to arrest him. The ranger kept his hand on his holster as if preparing to draw his service weapon, Perkins said, and the BLM manager told the sheriff he felt his life was in danger.

In a more documented case, BLM law enforcement clashed with civilian colleagues in Garfield County over a dead body.

Love and a team of FBI agents unearthed human remains discovered in the national monument in 2008, reasoning the site could be a crime scene. The monument archaeologist objected, however, believing the site was likely historic and any excavation should have been led by scientists.

The archaeologist was baffled that law enforcement did not notify him of their plans, and that Love failed to return his phone calls, according to BLM documents obtained through a records request.

The archaeologist was excluded as the cops dug up the body with a TV crew filming. The remains turned out to be that of an American Indian who died in the 19th century.

All sides agree better cooperation would minimize such disagreements and make the job of law enforcement easier. The challenge will be re-establishing trust.

———

It may seem improbable that a single officer could become so notorious, but hearings right here in this committee have confirmed that the BLM is able to ignore the authority of local sheriffs and other elected officials without repercussions.

One county commissioner described their issues with BLM as "bullying, intimidation and a lack of integrity."

Appeals from the highest levels of the Utah state government were met with open ears from Bureau officials, but zero action was taken. This particular officer continues to make new friends and has popped up in the news again for his adoration of Choco Tacos and demands for superstar treatment at outdoor hippie festivals.

We could easily conclude that this was just one rogue officer and surely he will be dealt with, but that is not the case. If we have a system that allows this to continue, then these accountability issues will remain unchanged and repeated. In fact, I have heard surprising stories from local authorities and government officials in my own district regarding abuses or callous ignoring of the needs of local officials who have difficulty getting needed cooperation from Federal authorities in charge of land within their county.

Once we come to a better understanding of how these problems have been able to persist, we can move to a suitable corrective action. We have four witnesses today offering a variety of perspectives with experience we value. From their testimony we will hear how something in the implementation of this "stove-piping" of authority is foiling responsive, efficient, and accountable performance. I invite our witnesses to tell us how this can be better understood and addressed.

I am also concerned that Federal law enforcement have actively usurped state authority. I want to know how this occurs and how it must stop. Local sheriffs are elected and held accountable by their constituents. Regardless of the party in the White House, Federal officers' accountability only seems to be present if there is adequate congressional oversight and if congressional consequences exist for any impropriety. Even so, it is nearly impossible to dismiss a Federal employee.

At some point, we will welcome input from the Administration; but it is my understanding that they were unwilling to send representatives from the sub-agencies we requested to testify at this hearing. That type of callousness is the very type that we must either stop, or defund the noncompliant bureau, agency, or department.

Nevertheless, we will continue to dialog and look forward to uncovering ways to bring accountability to Federal law enforcement.

[The prepared statement of Mr. Gohmert follows:]

PREPARED STATEMENT OF THE HON. LOUIE GOHMERT, CHAIRMAN, SUBCOMMITTEE ON OVERSIGHT AND INVESTIGATIONS

Today we are discussing the accountability of law enforcement within our land management agencies. I'd like to recognize from the start the important work of hundreds of law enforcement employees from the Department of the Interior to the U.S. Forest Service. These men and women risk everything to protect our iconic landmarks, natural resources as well as critical energy infrastructure. Just last year, 38-year-old Forest Service Officer Jason Crisp and his K-9 partner were killed while pursuing an armed murder suspect. That was a horrible tragedy and his sacrifice should be remembered by all of us.

Clearly there are many, many excellent officers out there just doing their job day in and day out. Unfortunately, we have come to learn of situations that place *local* law enforcement officers at odds with their *Federal* counterparts.

I'd like to enter into the record an article from the *Salt Lake Tribune*, published in October of 2014, entitled "Utah to BLM: Rein in Your Cops." The article begins, "Public Enemy No. 1 for rural Utah sheriffs just happens to be a fellow peace officer: Dan Love, the Bureau of Land Management's special agent in charge."

It may seem improbable that a single officer could become so notorious, but hearings right here in this committee confirmed that the BLM is able to ignore the authority of local sheriffs and other elected officials without repercussions. One county commissioner described their issues with BLM as "bullying, intimidation and lack of integrity." Appeals from the highest levels of the Utah state government were met with open ears from bureau officials, but zero action was taken. This particular officer continues to make new friends and has popped up in the news again for his adoration of Choco Tacos and demands for superstar treatment at outdoor hippie festivals.

We could easily conclude that this is just one rogue officer and surely he'll be dealt with. But that isn't the case. If we have a system that allows this to continue, then these accountability issues will remain unchanged and repeated.

In fact, I have heard surprising stories from local authorities or government officials in my district regarding abuses or the calloused ignoring of the needs of local officials who have difficulty getting needed cooperation from Federal authorities in charge of land within their county.

Once we come to a better understanding of how these problems have been able to persist, we can move to a suitable corrective action. We have four witnesses today offering a variety of perspectives with experience we value. From their testimony we will hear how something in the implementation of this "stove-piping" of authority is foiling responsive, efficient and accountable performance. I invite our witnesses to tell us how this can be better understood and addressed.

I'm also concerned that Federal law enforcement have actively usurped state authority. I want to know how this occurs and how it must stop. Local sheriffs are *elected* and held accountable by their constituents. Regardless of the party in the White House, Federal officers' accountability only seems to be present if there is adequate congressional oversight, and congressional consequences for any impropriety. Even so, it is nearly impossible to dismiss a Federal employee.

At some point we will welcome input from the Administration, but it is my understanding they were unwilling to send representatives from the sub-agencies we requested to testify at this hearing. That type of callousness is the very type that we must either stop, or defund the non-compliant bureau, agency, or department. Nevertheless, we will continue to dialog and look forward to uncovering ways to bring accountability to Federal law enforcement.

———

Mr. GOHMERT. At this time I would like to call upon our Ranking Member, Mrs. Dingell, for her opening statement.

STATEMENT OF THE HON. DEBBIE DINGELL, A REPRESENTATIVE IN CONGRESS FROM THE STATE OF MICHIGAN

Mrs. DINGELL. Good morning and thank you, Mr. Chairman.

I want to give my thanks to all the witnesses this morning for taking the time and the trouble to testify, and I want to give particular thanks to Sheriff Brown and Mr. Schoppmeyer for their service.

Law enforcement within Federal land management agencies is no easy task. Conservation law enforcement officers face challenges that are significantly different than those faced by non-conservation law enforcement. The breadth of the crimes that they confront and the laws that they enforce are unlike any other.

As the Chairman has raised, there may be some problems; but we need to respect and understand the importance of what law enforcement is doing in these conservation areas.

A study of the crimes confronted by the Forest Service law enforcement officers found that they fall into three categories. The first is urban-associated crime, which includes arson, body dumping, gang activity, and other types of criminal behavior.

The second is drug activity, like armed defense of marijuana cultivation on Forest Service land, or methamphetamine labs—that is always a hard word.

The third is violence perpetrated by members of extremist and nontraditional groups, like satanic cults, survivalists, and militia/supremacy groups. These groups are tough.

The law enforcement officers there protect the resources we depend on every day and provide for public safety. While these officers' mandates are unique, the officers and the work that they do is under attack.

We will hear today about a proposal to weaken enforcement mechanisms for the Lacey Act by decriminalizing it, despite the use of illegally harvested plant or animal products, like ivory, to fund terrorist groups.

Like I do every night before our hearings, I was doing my late night study. The Chairman raised the issue of "stove-piping." So I learned last night that it was instituted after years of pressure from watchdogs and Congress and was implemented to make Forest Service law enforcement more effective, fair, and independent.

So I want to make sure, as we are looking at it, that we are fair and objective on all of it, while I recognize that there may be issues.

And we will hear about the FOCUS Act, which would remove the ability for the Fish and Wildlife Service and NOAA enforcement officers to carry firearms.

The work performed by land management agency law enforcement is just as challenging, just as important, and just as dangerous as other law enforcement jobs. These Americans put their lives on the line whenever they report for work in an effort to protect us and our natural resources.

The Chairman mentioned Jason Crisp. I want to talk more in detail about him. Before starting with the U.S. Forest Service as a law enforcement officer in 2004, Jason Crisp served with the McDowell County Sheriff's Office in North Carolina for 7 years. He developed a reputation as a selfless person who was eager to provide assistance.

In 2014, Officer Crisp was investigating the case of a couple found dead in their home. There was evidence of a struggle and a missing vehicle. Police soon began to suspect that the couple's son was the killer. Over 100 officers from six agencies joined the manhunt. At about 3:00 p.m., the suspect purportedly ambushed Officer

Crisp and his K-9 partner. He shot the dog and Officer Crisp, took Crisp's gun, and kept running.

An Avery County Sheriff's Deputy, and troopers assigned to Burke County who were near the shooting, attempted to save Officer Crisp's life, but they were unable to.

Soon after, the suspect was found and refused to drop his weapon. The suspect died of a self-inflicted gunshot wound.

U.S. Forest Service Officer Jason Crisp is survived by his wife, Amanda and his sons, Garrett and Logan. He was 38 years old.

I hope as we undertake these hearings that we will always remember the contributions and sacrifices of our law enforcement officers.

I yield back the balance of my time.

[The prepared statement of Mrs. Dingell follows:]

PREPARED STATEMENT OF THE HON. DEBBIE DINGELL, RANKING MEMBER, SUBCOMMITTEE ON OVERSIGHT AND INVESTIGATIONS

Good morning and thank you, Mr. Chairman. I want to give my thanks to all the witnesses for taking the trouble to testify today. And I also want to thank both Sheriff Brown and Mr. Schoppmeyer for their service.

Law enforcement within Federal land management agencies is no easy task. Conservation law enforcement officers face challenges that are significantly different than those faced by non-conservation law enforcement. The breadth of crimes they confront and the laws they enforce are unlike any other.

A study of the crimes confronted by Forest Service law enforcement officers found that they fall into three categories. The first is urban-associated crime, which includes arson, body dumping, gang activity, and other types of criminal behavior. The second is drug activity, like armed defense of marijuana cultivation on forest service land, or methamphetamine labs. The third is violence perpetrated by members of extremist and nontraditional groups like satanic cults, survivalists, and militia/supremacy groups. They protect the resources we depend on every day and provide for public safety.

While these officers' mandates are unique, the officers and the work they do is also under attack.

We will hear today about a proposal to weaken enforcement mechanisms for the Lacey Act by decriminalizing it, despite the use of illegally harvested plant or animal products like ivory to fund terrorist groups. We will hear about why we should remove a management structure called stove-piping that was instituted after years of pressure from watchdogs and Congress, and which was implemented to make Forest Service law enforcement more effective, fair, and independent. And we will hear about the FOCUS Act, which would remove the ability for Fish and Wildlife Service and NOAA enforcement officers to carry firearms.

The work performed by land management agency law enforcement is just as challenging, just as important, and just as dangerous as other law enforcement jobs. These Americans put their lives on the line whenever they report for work in an effort to protect us and our natural resources.

Before starting with the U.S. Forest Service as a law enforcement officer in 2004, Jason Crisp served with the McDowell County Sheriff's office in North Carolina for 7 years. He developed a reputation as a selfless person who was eager to provide assistance.

In 2014, Officer Crisp was investigating the case of a couple found dead in their home. There was evidence of a struggle and a missing vehicle. Police soon began to suspect the couple's son to be the killer. Over 100 officers from about six agencies joined the manhunt.

At about 3 p.m., the suspect reportedly ambushed Officer Crisp and his K-9 partner. He shot the dog and Officer Crisp, took Crisp's gun and kept running. An Avery County Sheriff's deputy and troopers assigned to Burke County, who were near the shooting, attempted to save Officer Crisp's life, but were unable. Soon after, the suspect was found and refused to drop his weapon. He died of a self-inflicted gunshot wound.

U.S. Forest Service Officer Jason Crisp is survived by his wife, Amanda, and his sons, Garrett and Logan. He was 38 years old.

I hope we will always remember the contributions and sacrifices of our law enforcement officers. I yield back my time.

Mr. GOHMERT. I thank the Ranking Member very much for her opening statement.

Now I will introduce the witnesses. We are very pleased that you arrived here, and have done so voluntarily; and obviously, you do not come for the big bucks because you do not even get reimbursed. That is why we appreciate so much your appearance here today, all four of you. Thank you.

First we have Sheriff Dave Brown of Skamania County, Washington. We also have Mr. Russ Ehnes, who is the Executive Director at the National Off-Highway Vehicle Conservation Council. Next is Mr. Christopher Schoppmeyer, who is the Vice President of Agency Affairs at the Federal Law Enforcement Officers Association. And finally, we have Mr. Paul Larkin, Jr., who is the Senior Legal Research Fellow with the Edwin Meese Center for Legal and Justice Studies at The Heritage Foundation.

Let me remind the witnesses that, under our Committee Rules, oral statements are limited to 5 minutes. You have a timer in front of you. Your written statements—I know that my colleague and I both do late night work in preparation, and we have read your statements. We are greatly appreciative of your written statements, and those will be entered as part of the record, regardless of whether you get that finished within 5 minutes or not. If you care to expand on that within your 5 minutes and bring up something that is not in the written testimony, it will still be part of the record.

When you begin the light on the witness table will be green. When you have 1 minute remaining, the yellow light will come on, and when your time has expired, the red light comes on. At that time it will be gaveled to complete.

So the Chair recognizes Sheriff Brown for your opening statement. You are recognized for 5 minutes, Sheriff. Thanks for being here.

STATEMENT OF DAVE BROWN, SHERIFF, SKAMANIA COUNTY, WASHINGTON

Sheriff BROWN. Thank you, Chairman Gohmert, Ranking Member Dingell, members of the committee.

I am here today to testify on behalf of the Western States Sheriffs' Association and the more than 800 sheriffs in the 15 states that we represent.

The nearly 200 million acres of Federal forestland managed by the U.S. Forest Service represents a national treasure of incredible value, the treasure of natural beauty and resources deserving sound management and protection. U.S. Forest Service has been tasked with that management and protection to include the dedicated law enforcement officers, or LEOs, who enforce resource protection laws.

With over 28 years of law enforcement experience in Skamania County, including 9 years patrolling the Gifford Pinchot National Forest, I routinely worked with district rangers and LEOs. The productive working relationships I developed in the late 1980s and early 1990s changed in 1993 when U.S. Forest Service law enforcement investigations became an independent entity under central direction from Washington, DC.

This restructuring, commonly called the "stove-pipe effect," took place just 1 year prior to the implementation of the Northwest Forest Plan. The effect of this over time has served only to distract LEOs from their primary responsibility of resource protection by shifting their focus to law enforcement functions traditionally addressed by county sheriffs.

Additional LEOs were added to patrol efforts. K-9 units and radar enforcement capabilities were added. Traffic enforcement off national forest system roads became common, and individuals were often arrested on state warrants.

Funding also provided to sheriffs for cooperative law enforcement contracts declined. It became evident the Forest Service law enforcement was no longer focused on resource protection. While Skamania County has no Bureau of Land Management, or BLM, managed land, sheriffs across the western states struggle with similar issues in witnessing the BLM migration away from resource protection.

These actions were recognized by county sheriffs as being outside the scope of authority and jurisdiction of both the Forest Service and the BLM.

The failure of the "stove-piping" of Forest Service law enforcement was the subject of a congressional hearing in 1998. The issues we are discussing here today are the same issues that were discussed without resolution 17 years ago.

There have, however, been some successes in the past 4 years. We began building stronger relationships with the Forest Service. The Western States Sheriffs' Association has worked together with the Director of Forest Service Law Enforcement and Investigations to create a Memorandum of Agreement, including a template when sheriffs are considering providing state authority to an LEO.

In the agreement, the Forest Service acknowledges the sheriff is the chief law enforcement officer in the county. As such, the sheriff is accountable and responsible to the citizens for promoting a law enforcement philosophy for their county, including our public lands. County sheriffs, the managers of Federal law enforcement agencies, and the public deserve a positive working relationship and open lines of communication.

I submit there are five immediate remedies to accomplish this.

First, eliminate the stove-pipe structure of the Forest Service law enforcement. Reintegrate the Special Agents in Charge and the LEOs into the regional and local structure to reconnect the Forest Service law enforcement with the county sheriff and the lands they protect.

Two, create a local law enforcement council chaired by the sheriff to include Forest Service and BLM representatives for effective local oversight.

Three, review the Code of Federal Regulation and eliminate language that assimilates state crimes or state statutes into Forest Service and BLM enforcement.

Four, examine staffing levels of the Forest Service and the BLM law enforcement agencies and align those levels to the management activities on the lands they protect.

Five, expand cooperative law enforcement agreements with the county sheriff.

While these hearings are important to expose the issues and openly debate them, right now is the time for action. Now is the time to take substantive steps to rebuild trust among sheriffs and our Federal partners.

I urge this committee to examine all of the written testimony. I am confident you will reach a course of action to improve our public safety services for all citizens who live near and/or visit our treasured national forestlands. It is they we all serve.

Thank you for your time, and I am available for questions.

[The prepared statement of Sheriff Brown follows:]

PREPARED STATEMENT OF SHERIFF DAVE BROWN, SKAMANIA COUNTY, WASHINGTON; PRESIDENT, WESTERN STATES SHERIFFS' ASSOCIATION

Mr. Chairman, Ranking Member Dingell, and members of the committee: my name is Dave Brown and I serve as the Sheriff in Skamania County in Washington State.

I am here today to testify on behalf of the Western States Sheriffs' Association, and more than 800 Sheriffs in the 15 states we represent.

The nearly 200 million acres of Federal land managed by the U.S. Forest Service represent a national treasure of incredible value. A treasure that deserves sound management and resource protection.

The U.S. Forest Service has been tasked with that protection, including the dedicated Law Enforcement Officers (LEOs) who enforce resource protection laws.

Historically those LEOs were assigned to the District Ranger and worked closely with local law enforcement, particularly the elected county Sheriffs. My nearly 29 years of law enforcement experience includes 9 years of patrolling the Gifford Pinchot National Forest in Washington State, where I routinely worked with LEOs and district rangers.

The productive working relationships I developed in the late 1980s and early 1990s saw a dramatic change after 1993 when USFS Law Enforcement and Investigations became an independent entity within the Forest Service, under central direction from Washington, DC. This restructuring has commonly been called the stove-pipe effect. The result of this restructuring quickly created a disconnect with local communities and, in essence, created a national police force.

The District Ranger and Forest Supervisor as well as the Regional Forester no longer had budgetary authority, supervisory or operational control over law enforcement activities on the forest. When this happened, the local county Sheriff had no incentive to meet with the District Ranger or Forest Supervisor to discuss operational objectives for law enforcement on national forest system lands within the county and expect any reasonable progress on addressing enforcement concerns. The negotiation of cooperative law enforcement agreements was no longer in the purview of the District Ranger as the stove-pipe provided that the Special Agent in Charge (SAC) was solely responsible for this effort. The SAC can often be responsible for oversight on multiple national forests spread out over as little as two states and sometimes across four to five states. The ability for a county Sheriff to have a strong working relationship with the SAC became an impossible task for most sheriffs due to distances between the Sheriff's Office and the forest headquarters where the SAC is assigned.

This stove-pipe served only to distract LEOs from their primary responsibility of resource protection by shifting their focus to other policing functions best left to local law enforcement. As time progressed through the 1990s and into the early 2000s, additional LEOs were added to the patrol efforts of the USFS and funding that was provided to Sheriffs for cooperative law enforcement contracts continued to decline.

Over time, the USFS law enforcement and investigations division began to add K–9 units and radar enforcement capabilities. Traffic enforcement both on and off National Forest System roads became a common occurrence. LEOs began seeking assistance from county Sheriffs to house arrestees on Federal charges in the local jail. It became evident in many counties across the West that the USFS law enforcement component was no longer focused on resource protection and timber related issues.

In some instances, LEOs began arresting individuals on state warrants and transporting them to the local jail. These actions were recognized by county Sheriffs as being outside the scope of authority and jurisdiction of the USFS law enforcement component.

Most western states only recognize a Federal LEO to have authority over Federal crimes on federally managed lands. It became apparent to sheriffs in many jurisdictions that some USFS LEOs were generating a multitude of citizen complaints. Those complaints were most often filed with the Sheriff. The Sheriff, having no supervisory authority over a Federal officer was obligated to pass the information on to a patrol captain or SAC. In many cases, there was never a response back or any apparent investigation into the actions of the LEO. I experienced this specific scenario in Skamania County throughout the late 1990s into the early 2000s. The point here is that there appeared to be no accountability within the structure of the USFS law enforcement component and no willingness to communicate with the local sheriff or the community regarding the actions of the LEOs. As these actions continued, citizens began to express concerns for their personal safety, feeling as if they were being harassed and targeted. While additional complaints were forwarded to the local supervisors and sometimes directly to the Washington Office, in my particular case, there appeared to be no desire to deal with the officers' actions.

This new order was, for all intents and purposes, a Federal police agency attempting to patrol and enforce the Code of Federal Regulation, a code that had been revised to assimilate state crimes in a manner that mirrors those responsibilities mandated to the county Sheriff.

This failure of the 'stove piping' of the USFS Law Enforcement and Investigations was the subject of a congressional hearing in 1998. A copy of that hearing has been submitted as a part of the written testimony and supporting documents packet. The very issues we are discussing today are the same issues that were discussed 17 years ago.

While I am aware the committee is seeking information from Sheriffs regarding BLM law enforcement, my county has no BLM managed land. I have, however, spent much time listening to Sheriffs across the other western states regarding similar issues. There are examples out of the state of Utah that illustrate a heavy handed approach by the BLM rangers and Special Agents in more than one case. The tactics and operations utilized in these cases go well beyond the boundaries of decent, professional and appropriate conduct of any law enforcement officer. There have been specific issues arising out of San Juan County, Utah that eventually led to the deaths of three citizens of that county. These were instances of suicide and one can argue that it was the result of the manner in which the BLM approached the case and how they interacted with those involved. These cases were related to the closure of a trail in the Recapture Canyon area of San Juan County Utah and an alleged artifacts theft case in San Juan County, Utah. These cases deserve review by Congress and should well articulate the lack of oversight and accountability of the part of the BLM law enforcement.

There should be no question as a matter of state statute as to who the Chief Law Enforcement Officer of the county is. The elected sheriff is responsible for determining the law enforcement philosophy of the unincorporated land mass of the county including our national forests lands.

There can be no argument that there are some county Sheriffs who do not recognize the USFS law enforcement as a legal and legitimate entity. Some go as far as to dispute the constitutional basis that allows this organization to exist. The Western States Sheriffs' Association does not dispute the legitimacy of the USFS law enforcement component but does hold the belief, based on state law, that the Sheriff is the Chief Law Enforcement Officer of the county.

That belief is firmly held by our membership. The county Sheriff, an elected representative of the people, is responsible for determining the law enforcement philosophy as it relates to the protection of life and property within their jurisdictional boundaries.

It should be stated that there have been many successes in the past 5 years. The Director of Law Enforcement and Investigations for the USFS has genuinely reached out to the Western Sheriffs since 2011. Together we have built a stronger working relationship with both the Director and the Deputy Director. There has been an ongoing effort to unite the Sheriffs across the West with the Special Agent in Charge responsible for the Federal law enforcement activities on the public lands in their county. It has been evident that recent complaints regarding the actions of individual LEOs are being heard now and in some cases there appears to be a concerted effort to address those complaints. The Western States Sheriffs' Association worked together with the Director to create a Memorandum of Understanding that provides a template for Sheriffs to use when considering providing state authority to a LEO. In the agreement, the USFS recognizes the Sheriff as the Chief Law enforcement Officer of the county. There is language that provides the ability to house Federal inmates at local jails and to incorporate LEOs into the Sheriffs training programs.

This philosophy should extend to all policing efforts on federally managed lands. This philosophy should be instilled into the leadership of the USFS and the BLM. We cannot serve the county residents and visitors who use our Nation's public lands when we are divided on the philosophy, method, and manner in which we treat the people we serve.

Both county Sheriffs and the managers of Federal law enforcement agencies deserve a positive working relationship and open lines of communications. I submit there are a number of effective remedies that must be considered:

1. The first of these remedies can be found in the recently signed Memorandum of Understanding (MOU) between the Western States Sheriffs' Association and the USFS Director of Law Enforcement and Investigations. This document calls for the creation of local Law Enforcement Councils (LECs). In this model, the county Sheriff chairs the Council which is comprised of adjoining county Sheriffs and local USFS law enforcement leadership. These LECs provide the greatest opportunity for open communication on a variety of issues and all occurs at the local level where it stands the best chance of being effective.

2. Eliminate the stove-pipe structure of the USFS LE&I. Reestablish the operational structure that inserts the Special Agent in Charge back under the supervision and direction of the Regional Forester. At the same time, put the LEOs back into the command structure of the local district ranger. By reintegrating the SAC and the LEOs into the regional and local structure, there will be a greater opportunity to reconnect USFS law enforcement with the county Sheriff and create the necessary local focus in order to conduct the important work of protecting our treasured National Forests.

3. Conduct a widespread review of the Code of Federal Regulation currently in use by USFS and BLM law enforcement. Every effort should be made to eliminate all language that assimilates state crime or state statutes into USFS and BLM enforcement. The enforcement of crimes against persons and personal property crimes is, and should continue to be, the primary role of the county Sheriff.

4. Examine the staffing levels of the USFS and BLM law enforcement agencies. It is the belief of the Western States Sheriffs that the LEO and Ranger positions are across the two agencies could be reduced. The costs savings recognized through the reduction should be distributed back to the county Sheriff through the cooperative law enforcement agreements. This additional funding would potentially allow the county Sheriff a better ability to respond to and investigate criminal activity on our public lands.

While it seems we have made progress in alleviating some concerns of Western Sheriffs, we continue to be vigilant to ensure there is no expansion of authority and that the USFS law enforcement continues to recognize the authority and responsibility of the county Sheriff.

The Sheriff is chosen by the people of the county to serve as their elected law enforcement representative. The people did not choose the Forest Service or the Bureau of Land Management for this function. If the local sheriff desires the assistance of the Federal law enforcement officers, there is a mechanism in place to accomplish this. Sheriffs, under state statute, have the authority to cross-deputize LEOs. As mentioned earlier, this can also be accomplished through MOUs such as the one in place now.

The health of our national forests has been on the decline for the past 20 years. Since the implementation of the Northwest Forest Plan the annual timber harvests on National Forest lands in the Pacific Northwest has dropped dramatically. This effect has led to a decline in local economies, a reduction in local and state government services, and has had a severe impact on public safety services in many counties across the West.

Is it merely a coincidence that in 1993 the stove-pipe structure for USFS Law Enforcement was created? Perhaps it was intentional that this was done in order to protect the jobs of the law enforcement officers within the agency. Traditionally funded through timber receipts and general appropriations, the law enforcement division was now its own entity and no longer dependent on timber harvests. This would prove to be beneficial for the LE&I division considering the decline in timber funds after the Northwest Forest Plan was implemented. Since that time, the ability of the Forest Service to carry out its mission has declined and many positions have been lost due to lack of funding. At the same time, the law enforcement division has expanded, creating more positions and increasing their budget for many years.

The original function of resource protection and timber related criminal investigations were no longer the priority due to decline in management of our national forests. However, the desire to morph into a traditional police force has been realized and perpetrated in counties across the West. It is possible this stove-pipe structure was intentionally carried out to preserve and grow the USFS law enforcement component during a time when the normal, recognized functions of the agency were and have continued to suffer.

While these hearings are important in order to expose the issues and openly debate them, right now is a time for action. Now is the time to take a substantial step to rebuild trusts among Sheriffs and our Federal partners. Now is the time to truly evaluate the levels of enforcement capabilities of our national forests law enforcement providers and to finally realize that the county Sheriff is in the best position, from a matter of law, to effectively deal with crime on our Nation's forest. I urge this committee to take the time to review all of the written testimony. I am hopeful that you will recognize and appreciate our position and reach out to our leadership and the USFS law enforcement leaders. By doing so, we will continue to have opportunities to dialog with each other and hopefully reach consensus regarding a course of action that improves our public safety services to citizens who recreate and visit our national forestlands.

Attachment

*****

Supporting Documentation Provided by Kane County Utah Sheriff Tracy Glover

I am the Sheriff of Kane County Utah. I have about 4,000 square miles that borders Arizona to the south. I have about 90 percent Federal land in my county including the Dixie National Forest, part of Bryce Canyon National Park, Zion National Park, Glen Canyon National Recreation Area and the Grand Staircase Escalante National Monument. I regularly work with Federal law enforcement including the U.S. Forest Service, the BLM and the National Park Service. I have been in Law enforcement for the past 18 years. I took office as the elected Sheriff January 5, 2015 after serving as the Undersheriff for Sheriff Lamont Smith for 15 years. The comments shared in this document are my opinions based on my own personal experiences.

I could tell many sad war stories but I think it is more useful to discuss the broad issues in order to solve the broad problem.

I think it is important to start with the basics in Federal law enforcement. We must always discuss jurisdiction separate from authority.

We must separate the agencies instead of making the common mistake of lumping them all together under the "Federal law enforcement" label.

Authority

The USFS, BLM and National Park Service each have law enforcement divisions that are unique and different in their roles and responsibilities. Each Agency has been created by some piece of enabling legislation that lays out the legislative intent of Congress at the time of their creation. Each respective piece of enabling legislation is where the individual agency draws their unique law enforcement authority.

Jurisdiction

The National Park Service works under three types of jurisdiction: Exclusive (Yellowstone, Yosemite, etc.); Concurrent (Grand Canyon, etc.); and Proprietary (Zion National Park, Bryce Canyon National Park, Glen Canyon NRA, etc.).

The USFS and the BLM only work under proprietary jurisdiction, which is limited in scope to the basic jurisdiction of a landowner. As opposed to exclusive and concurrent jurisdictions, the scope of proprietary Jurisdiction does not include Federal criminal enforcement or prosecution and does not allow the assimilative crimes act (18 U.S.C. 13) to be used for the Federal prosecution of assimilated state crimes.

It is important that sheriffs, legislators, upper level managers and cabinet officials understand that not all Federal agencies are created equal. Federal agency philosophies must be adjusted to fit the type of authority and jurisdiction each respective agency is working under.

Because I am aware of your vast knowledge of USFS practices, I am going to focus my comments toward the BLM.

The Problem(s)

Over the past 15 years, the law enforcement philosophies of the BLM seem to be transforming at a rapid pace. I would only be speculating if I were to state where the changes are being driven from, but there is no question that there have been marked changes. One explanation might be a response to the designation of large tracts of land under the BLM's management as National Monuments. Another might simply be a new and more aggressive philosophy that arrived with personnel changes in the upper levels of law enforcement within the BLM. Either way, we as sheriffs have good reason to be concerned with the duplication of our traditional duties. What used to be a routine call to the county sheriff is often a call to a Federal LEO. What used to be a handful of friendly Federal rangers protecting natural resources has now turned into thigh-rigs, riot gear, Federal K-9 units and tactical teams with POLICE written down their sleeves and on their backs. Line managers are now encouraged to only call the Sheriff as a last resort and to rely on rangers as much as possible.

Across Utah, successful long-term law enforcement contracts were cut with no reasonable explanation. We were told that the BLM State Director wanted to keep the contracts in place, as did the local BLM managers, the sheriffs and county commissioners. We were told that the decision to cut the contracts was made by the Special Agent in Charge and were not given any opportunity to revise practices or review the scope of work.

Since Bill Woody resigned as the director of law enforcement for the BLM, trust between rural Utah sheriffs and BLM LEO leaders has eroded significantly. There have been a series of botched law enforcement raids, protest events and public meetings that have undermined the Sheriff's role in his community all across southern Utah and Nevada. There are many solid officers that work under the BLM, USFS and NPS umbrella. Public trust for the men and women that serve in BLM law enforcement is at an all time low. Sheriff's are constantly being urged to step up and exercise our authority as the lead law enforcement agent in the county. The aggressive change in philosophy on the Federal level continues to cause state, local and Federal relationships to struggle. And the sad thing is that it does not have to be this way.

The Solution

If possible, we must find our way back to a place where the Federal agencies have unwavering confidence in their local sheriff. I often remind the folks at my local BLM office that I am their sheriff too. We must convince the Federal LEO leaders that we are not a threat to them but instead we are passionate about fulfilling our statutory responsibilities as the County Sheriff. We are proud of what we do and we want them to be proud to be forest rangers, park rangers and BLM rangers. Resource protection is what they signed up for. It should not feel degrading for them to pass along law enforcement duties to us. Their reluctance to rely on us is a learned behavior. As sheriffs we are willing to work together in partnerships as long as we all respect the traditional law enforcement roles that have been successful for hundreds of years. The philosophy of BLM law enforcement should be adjusted from the aggressive and confrontational style that is becoming more common, to more of a focus back on resource management. Coordination and cooperation with the local sheriff in all law enforcement matters should be the ultimate goal and Federal LEO personnel should be made to feel comfortable in doing so. Line managers should also be encouraged to coordinate and cooperate with their local sheriff regarding needs and concerns that exist in their respective management areas. Contracts for additional local law enforcement should be reviewed and offered where appropriate, effective, efficient and desirable. The intent of Congress in FLPMA to achieve maximum feasible reliance on local law enforcement is pretty clear. This concept should be the shared desire of sheriffs and Federal agencies alike.

It has been my experience that when this model is followed, problems cease to exist and progress is sure to follow. I have never been more frustrated than when my BLM contract was cut and my local manager was not sure whether he could still call me or not. It took years and great effort to develop the successful, effective relationship that existed and only one poor decision to call it into question.

What we need is simple shift in the aggressive philosophy and newly established practices of Federal law enforcement personnel accompanied by some good old-fashioned effort on the part of the county sheriffs.

Sheriff Tracy Glover
Kane County Utah

Additional Supporting Material for the Record; Submitted on Behalf of Sheriff Tracy Glover, Kane County, Utah

When I mentioned "an aggressive change in philosophy on the Federal level continues to cause state, local and Federal relationships to struggle" I was referring to both the appetite for expansion within BLM law enforcement as well as specific experiences we have shared over the past several years. It seems that the goal is to have enough BLM law enforcement to handle POLICE issues on public lands without the need to involve the local Sheriff. I believe it is mandatory under the rules of FLPMA that the BLM "achieve maximum feasible reliance on local law enforcement" and this concept is what I would like to get back to.

Over the past 15 years, the management of BLM lands has taken on a much different look in Southern Utah and Northern Arizona. As national monuments have been created and resource and travel management plans have been amended, closures and restrictions have been steadily increasing. Tensions have also increased as people feel they are losing their access and heritage. Counties have pursued litigation to protect rights of way which has created the appearance of an adversarial relationship between entities.

Through all of this, my BLM experience on a local level has been mostly positive. Somewhat surprisingly, we have managed to maintain a very successful law enforcement contract with local BLM officials. We have been very responsive to their needs and they have developed great confidence in the Sheriff's Office. Even with that, there have been times during the contract years that BLM law enforcement seemed threatened by our ability to work with our local managers. What was once a relaxed relationship based on a level of respect for the Office of Sheriff shifted to a strained relationship with BLM law enforcement management.

Example:

On one occasion, I was made aware of a OHV protest and counter protest that was to occur on the Grand Staircase Escalante National Monument (GSENM) in Kane County. After contacting the leaders of both sides and in the spirit of coordination, cooperation and mutual respect, I contacted the GSENM office in Kanab. I had short notice as the ride was set for Saturday morning. I set up a meeting with the monument manager and upper management as well as law enforcement officials on the previous Thursday. The meeting was joined telephonically by officials from the BLM State Office. I informed the group of the intent of both sides of the protest. I told them of my meetings with both leaders and that I had laid out ground rules to keep the conflict peaceful. I was completely forthcoming with them and asked that they hold back the BLM law enforcement presence as I was assembling a large contingent of deputies to handle any problems and conflicts that might arise. Everyone at the table and on the phone agreed that this would be the proper approach agreeing that adding BLM law enforcement may escalate the situation.

By the next day, I received a phone call from a BLM law enforcement official stating that the U.S. Attorney wanted them to document the activity at the protest and stating that they would have a few plain clothes investigators present with cameras. I thought this was reasonable and agreed that we would watch for them and work with them as needed. Then Friday evening at about 9:00 p.m., I received a call from a BLM investigator informing me that they had changed their minds and that they were going to have a large contingent of uniformed BLM rangers present for the protest. I felt completely undermined and wished I had never contacted the BLM in the first place. As Saturday morning came, BLM rangers and investigators showed up. Some of them were wearing tactical gear with POLICE written down their sleeves and across their backs. At least one of them was wearing his handgun in a tactical thigh holster with many extra magazines exposed. All were holding cameras and photographing each protestor as they passed on the road. It was then that I first asked myself, when did the BLM rangers become the POLICE?

There have been a few other recent examples of BLM law enforcement officers gearing up in tactical gear and taking POLICE action. Some of these have been highly publicized. There are many BLM law enforcement rangers that I have worked closely with and have great respect for. These officers understand their role in the system and respect the other disciplines that are in place. I continue to be concerned that the selection and training processes employed by the BLM is now centered around a more hardcore, tactically capable, police officer rather than a friendly ranger who's primary reason for signing up was to protect the resource managed by the agency.

Relationships have remained solid between my office and local land managers while strained with BLM law enforcement leaders. At one point, about 3 years ago, the BLM elected to discontinue all law enforcement contracts in Utah. There is much speculation about why this happened but the bottom line is that it was a very unfortunate move. BLM managers have complained about the lack of contracts, Sheriff's have complained, County Commissioners have complained as well as state elected officials. For me, the contracts were much more than a quality service for a discounted fee. The contracts represented the ability for the BLM to rely on the local Sheriff for law enforcement services and that is just what they accomplished. Shortly after cutting the contracts, the BLM expanded their law enforcement division to include a mid level law enforcement regional manager.

I would like to see the law enforcement leadership within the BLM shift their philosophy. I would like to get back to a place where they recognize the sheriff as the law enforcement official in the county. I would like to see BLM law enforcement leadership genuinely come from a position of support for the County Sheriff and follow the direction in FLPMA in achieving maximum feasible reliance without feeling like it threatens their position. I would like to see less of a tactical, hard core BLM officer hired and trained but instead, a friendly ranger that knows he/she can call on the Sheriff to provide whatever level of law enforcement is needed at any given time. Every sheriff has access to the tactical resources and technical assets that may be required to handle any law enforcement incident within our respective counties. We are happy to step up and do our jobs even when it is awkward.

Sincerely,

SHERIFF TRACY GLOVER,
Kane County Sheriff's Office.

*****

The following item was submitted by Sheriff Brown for the record and will be retained in the Committee's official files:

—Transcript of June 23, 1998 Oversight Hearing on Forest Service Law Enforcement, Subcommittee on Forest and Forest Health

———————

Mr. GOHMERT. Thank you very much, Sheriff. I appreciate that statement.

At this time we will now hear from Mr. Ehnes. You are recognized to testify for 5 minutes, sir.

Thank you.

STATEMENT OF RUSS EHNES, EXECUTIVE DIRECTOR, NATIONAL OFF-HIGHWAY VEHICLE CONSERVATION COUNCIL, GREAT FALLS, MONTANA

Mr. EHNES. Mr. Chairman, Ranking Member, and members of the committee, thank you for the opportunity to testify on the accountability, policies, and tactics of law enforcement within the Department of the Interior and the U.S. Forest Service.

My name is Russ Ehnes, and I am the Executive Director of the National Off-Highway Vehicle Conservation Council, or NOVCC. We are a 501(c)(3), nonprofit, educational foundation. We have a 25-year history of working in partnership with the U.S. Forest Service to improve the management of off-highway vehicles' opportunities nationwide.

Through that period, NOVCC has conducted dozens of off-highway vehicle management workshops across the Nation in every Forest Service region. We have also published a book entitled, *Management Guidelines for Off-Highway Vehicle Recreation*; and we will soon release a comprehensive off-highway vehicle trail design, construction, maintenance and management guidebook.

The common theme in all of these workshops and publications is the "four E's," and the "four E's" are engineering, education, enforcement, and evaluation. The concept is simple. If managers apply proper engineering to trails and facilities, educate the public about how to use them responsibly, use enforcement when needed to address compliance issues, and evaluate the results and make adjustments, then OHV use will be successfully managed, sustainable, and fun.

The "four E's" are a simple and proven technique, and it has resulted in high quality, sustainable off-highway vehicle recreation opportunities across the Nation.

NOVCC is a strong proponent of enforcement, which is one of the "four E's" and one of the most important tools in the land manager's toolbox. Enforcement is critical not only for compliance, but is also an important educational tool. Not every encounter with the public results in a citation, nor should it.

Enforcement also contributes to visitor safety and to visitor sense of security while recreating on public lands. For the off-highway vehicle community, issues arise when the Forest Service supervisor and the district rangers cannot use enforcement to augment their management programs.

My personal example is similar to examples that NOVCC hears about across the country. I am currently the President of the Great Falls Trail Bike Riders Association, or GFTBRA. We have a very robust and successful partnership with the Lewis and Clark National Forest. GFTBRA contributes hundreds of hours of volunteer work every year, has a dozen certified sawyers, and employ two full-time seasonal workers to maintain trails. We've published over 80,000 maps in partnership with the U.S. Forest Service. The result is one of the best managed trail systems in the country.

In spite of these efforts, we still have compliance issues on holiday weekends in several locations. The few people causing the problems tend to be less involved in clubs. They're typically very casual users who show up once or twice a year on a holiday weekend and ride near campgrounds illegally. We know where they will be. We know when they will be there, and we know what they will be doing. Several years ago we asked the Forest Supervisor for help. We asked him to have the enforcement officers visit three key areas at key times.

He agreed that the timing was right and that the need for enforcement was critical, but could not promise that it would happen since he was not sure that this would be the top priority for his law enforcement person. He could only ask to see if it was the top priority of his LEO.

I mentioned we have a very strong partnership with the Lewis and Clark National Forest. Several years ago, we had a GFTBRA sponsored trail ride that was permitted in the Little Belt Mountains. At those rides, we inspect each and every vehicle to make sure they are in compliance with state sound limits, spark arresters, and to make sure that each vehicle is registered with its OHV decal. We also require the participants to wear helmets even though it is not required by state law.

Unbeknownst to us at that ride, and also unbeknownst to the recreation planner that we had worked with to coordinate the event, the U.S. Forest Service LEO set up a check station on a route leading into and out of the event. He did not issue any citations. Everyone was legal. However, the level of trust that we had worked to build with the Forest Service was damaged. Many of the riders wondered, "Why didn't the LEO just stop at our staging area to check us?" Many riders felt ambushed.

The issue is pretty simple as I see it. Forest supervisors are charged with managing national forests, and one of the most important tools in their toolbox is not dependably at their disposal. While cooperation between the supervisors and the law enforcement officer is generally the rule, it is the exception that causes problems for our community.

[The prepared statement of Mr. Ehnes follows:]

PREPARED STATEMENT OF RUSS EHNES, EXECUTIVE DIRECTOR, NATIONAL OFF-HIGHWAY VEHICLE CONSERVATION COUNCIL (NOHVCC)

Mr. Chairman, Ranking Member and members of the committee, thank you for this opportunity to testify on the Accountability, Policies, and Tactics of Law Enforcement within the Department of the Interior and the U.S. Forest Service.

My name is Russ Ehnes and I'm the Executive Director of the National Off-Highway Vehicle Conservation Council or NOHVCC. NOHVCC is a 501c3 non-profit educational foundation with a 25-year history of working in partnership with the U.S. Forest Service to improve management of off-highway vehicle opportunities nationwide. Through that period NOHVCC has conducted dozens of Off-Highway Vehicle Management Workshops across the Nation in every Forest Service Region. We have also published a book entitled, *Management Guidelines for OHV Recreation* and will soon release a comprehensive OHV trail design, construction and maintenance guidebook.

The common theme in all these workshops and publications is the "four E's," which are Engineering, Education, Enforcement, and Evaluation. The concept is simple: if managers apply proper engineering to trails and facilities, educate the public about how to use them responsibly, use enforcement when needed to address compliance issues, and evaluate the results and make adjustments, OHV use will be successfully managed, sustainable and fun. The "four E's" are simple and proven and have resulted in high-quality, sustainable OHV opportunities across the country.

NOHVCC is a strong proponent of enforcement, which is one of the "four E's" and one of the most important tools in the land manager's toolbox. Enforcement is critical not only for compliance but is also an important educational tool. Not every encounter with the public results in a citation, nor should it. Enforcement also contributes to visitor safety and the visitor's sense of security while recreating on our public lands.

For the OHV community, issues arise when the Forest Supervisor and District Rangers can't use enforcement to augment their management programs. My personal example is similar to other examples that NOHVCC hears about across the country.

I'm currently the President of the Great Falls Trail Bike Riders Association or GFTBRA. We have a very robust and successful partnership with the Lewis and Clark National Forest. GFTBRA contributes hundreds of hours of volunteer work, has a dozen certified sawyers, employs two full-time seasonal workers to maintain trails, and publishes maps in partnership with the USFS. The result is one of the best managed trail systems in the country.

In spite of all these efforts, we still have compliance issues on holiday weekends in several locations. The few people causing the problems tend to be less involved in clubs. They are typically casual users who only ride once or twice a year on holiday weekends and ride near campgrounds illegally.

We know where they will be, we know when they will be there, and we know what they will be doing. Several years ago we asked the Forest Supervisor for help. We asked him to have the enforcement officers visit three key areas at key times. He agreed that the timing was right and that the need for enforcement was critical but couldn't promise that it would happen since he wasn't sure that this would be the top priority for his law enforcement people. He could only ask to see if his top priority was also the top priority of the Law Enforcement Officers.

As I mentioned, GFTBRA has a strong partnership with the Lewis and Clark National Forest. Several years ago GFTBRA sponsored a permitted trail ride in the Little Belt Mountains. We inspect each vehicle for sound limit and spark arrester compliance and to be sure each vehicle has an OHV decal. We also require helmet use even though it is not required by law. Unbeknownst to us and the recreation planners we worked with to coordinate the permit and event, the USFS Law Enforcement Officer set up a check station on a route leading into and out of the event. He issued no citations. Everyone was legal. However, the level of trust we had built with the local Forest Service managers was damaged. Riders wondered "why the LEO wouldn't just stop at our staging area to check us?" Many riders felt "ambushed."

The issue as I see it is pretty simple. Forest Supervisors are charged with managing our National Forests and one of the most important tools in their toolbox is not dependably at their disposal. While cooperation between the Supervisors and the Law Enforcement Officers is generally the rule, it is the exception that causes problems for the OHV community.

———

Mr. GOHMERT. Thank you. I appreciate your testimony.

At this time we will hear from Mr. Schoppmeyer. You are recognized for 5 minutes for testimony.

STATEMENT OF CHRISTOPHER SCHOPPMEYER, VICE PRESIDENT FOR AGENCY AFFAIRS, FEDERAL LAW ENFORCEMENT OFFICERS ASSOCIATION, WASHINGTON, DC

Mr. SCHOPPMEYER. Thank you, Chairman Gohmert, Ranking Member Dingell, and members of the Subcommittee on Oversight and Investigations.

Good morning, and thank you for the opportunity to provide testimony relative to this hearing.

My name is Chris Schoppmeyer. My retirement last year marked 34 years of service as a Federal law enforcement officer. My service to the country included time in the U.S. Fish and Wildlife Service as a wildlife inspector and refuge law enforcement officer and as Special Agent within NOAA, National Marine Fishery Service, Office of Enforcement.

I also served in local government for 25 years as a conservation commissioner and then chairman of the town's Forensic Oversight Committee for the town of Newmarket, New Hampshire.

This provides me with decades of experience with local government issues and conservation issues. I understand and can talk about the Federal land use and law enforcement issues from both Federal and local government perspectives.

In addition to my government work, I serve as the Vice President for Agency Affairs for the Federal Law Enforcement Officers Association, where I created the Federal Law Enforcement Officers Association Environmental and Natural Resource Working Group composed of all land management agencies in the Departments of the Interior and Agriculture, as well as the Environmental Protection Agency and the NOAA Fishery Service Office of Enforcement. This working group was created to address agency and legislative issues specific to nontraditional law enforcement.

With regards to my testimony, I am going to address three points that directly and adversely affect our members who are Federal law enforcement officers from the Forest Service, BLM, the U.S. Fish and Wildlife Service, National Park Service, and the Environmental Protection Agency, Criminal Investigation Division.

The first issue I will address is the need for expanded use of off-highway recreational vehicle use on our national forests and other public lands. The use of the OHRVs has skyrocketed in recent years to include the use of seasonal machines, such as snowmobiles. This increase has been documented on both state, county, and local lands, as well as private lands.

In many states you must attend and successfully pass the mandatory OHRV course before you can legally operate an OHRV on any lands. OHRVs provide access to environmentally sensitive and designated wilderness tracts that are set aside to protect flora and fauna species that are in decline or at risk of becoming imperiled or extinct.

The use of checkpoints applies to all OHRV users, regardless of their being permitted or not. The fact is that the use of the checkpoint is not limited to just the permit; it involves checking for proper safety equipment, awareness of regulations specific to the area, and safe operation of the OHRV for the protection of the rider and the public in the area. This could include detecting individuals who may be operating an OHRV or snowmobile under the influence of alcohol or narcotics.

Expansion of OHRVs on our national forests and other public lands presents other problems for the scarce number of Forest Service officers, whose uniformed officer numbers have decreased from 750 FTEs to less than 450 officers, according to senior managers of the Forest Service LE&I.

The cultivation of marijuana groves in remote locations by DTOs, namely the Mexican cartel and other elements of organized crime, have significantly increased over the past decade, with evidence of marijuana groves being discovered as far north as the Upper Peninsula of Michigan.

The expanded use of OHRVs is already negatively impacting both public and private lands. I cite my home state of New Hampshire where OHRV regulations are enforced by conservation officers of New Hampshire Fish and Game. Despite the requirement of successful completion of the OHRV course, the number of fatalities increases and compliance is still an issue.

The second issue I will discuss just briefly is how dangerous conservation law enforcement is. Conservation law enforcement officers are nine times more likely to be assaulted with a dangerous weapon than traditional police officers. I only have to cite the two examples that the Ranking Member already did; and for the sake of time, I will only briefly mention that Officer Jason Crisp and his K-9, Maros, were brutally murdered in North Carolina.

The same on January 1, 2012. The National Park Service Law Enforcement Ranger Margaret Anderson was shot and killed while attempting to stop a fleeing suspect in Mount Rainier National Park. Unbeknownst to her, he was already wanted for serious felony crimes in the Seattle, Washington area.

The last point that I would like to discuss is on the regulations. I will address the premise that the Forest Service regulations do not require intent when violating, and result in over-criminalization of these regulations. Whether knowingly or unknowingly violating Forest Service regulations is the basis for enforcement action, it is usually based on the facts at hand, observations made, previous violation patterns, and the discretion of the Forest Service officer as to the level of action imposed.

The majority of regulatory offenses are petty in nature, but can range from a verbal warning to an arrest in the most extreme cases.

What I would suggest here, Mr. Chairman, is that—in my part, in the eastern side of the United States, we have very good relations between Federal, state, county, and local. I cite the other day a carry-out by New Hampshire Fish and Game in the White Mountain National Forest where we had the cooperation of the Forest Service, the Carroll County Sheriff's Department, and Pinkham Notch Rescue Squad. We had all of these local volunteers and, I have to say, that it is really astounding to me that we have such problems out West.

That concludes my testimony and I'm happy to take any questions you have. Thank you, sir.

[The prepared statement of Mr. Schoppmeyer follows:]

PREPARED STATEMENT OF CHRIS J. SCHOPPMEYER, VICE PRESIDENT FOR AGENCY AFFAIRS, FEDERAL LAW ENFORCEMENT OFFICERS ASSOCIATION

Chairman Gohmert, Ranking Member Dingell, and members of the Subcommittee on Oversight and Investigations, good morning and thank you for the opportunity to provide you testimony relative to this hearing.

My name is Chris Schoppmeyer and I am the Federal Law Enforcement Officers Association, Vice President for Agency Affairs. I have served in this position as a National Officer for 7½ years. During my tenure I created the FLEOA Environmental & Natural Resources Working Group composed of all the Land Management agencies in the Department of Interior, as well as the Environmental Protection Agency and NOAA Fisheries Service, and the U.S. Forest Service within the Department of Agriculture. This Working Group was created to address agency and legislative issues specific to non-traditional law enforcement.

I mandatorily retired at age 57 in February of 2014, after having served for 33½ years in Federal fisheries & wildlife law enforcement with both the U.S. Fish & Wildlife Service and NOAA Fisheries Service. I also served in local government of 25 years as Conservation Commissioner and then Chairman of the Forensic Oversight Committee for the town of Newmarket, New Hampshire, which provides me with decades of experience in local government conservation issues. I understand and can talk about Federal land use and law enforcement issues from both the Federal and local government perspectives.

Concerning my testimony, I am going to address several points that directly and adversely effect our members from the U.S. Forest Service, Bureau of Land Management, U.S. Fish & Wildlife Service, National Park Service and the Environmental Protection Agency.

The first issue I will address is the use of Off High Recreational Vehicles (OHRV) on our National Forests and other public lands. The use of OHRVs has sky rocketed in recent years to include the seasonal use of snowmobiles. This increase has been documented on both state, county and local lands as well as private lands. In many states you must attend and successfully pass a mandatory OHRV course before you can legally operate an OHRV on any lands. OHRVs provide access to environmentally sensitive areas and designated wilderness tracts that are set aside to protect species of flora and fauna that are in decline or at risk of becoming imperiled or extinct.

As a regular method employed to ensure the safety of all public land participants, the use of checkpoints applies to all OHRV users, regardless of their being permitted or not. The fact is that the use of a checkpoint is not limited to just the permit, it involves checking for the proper safety equipment, awareness of regulations specific to the area and safe operation of the OHRV for the protection of the rider and the public in the area. This could include detecting individuals who maybe operating an OHRV or snowmobile under the influence of alcohol or narcotics.

Expansion of OHRVs on National Forests and other public lands presents other problems for the scarce number of Forest Service Officers, whose uniformed officer numbers have been decreased from 750 FTEs to less than 450 officers, according to senior managers at the Forest Service LE&I.

The cultivation of marijuana groves in remote locations by Drug Trafficking Organizations (DTO) namely the Mexican cartel and other elements of organized crime has increased significantly over the past decade, with evidence of marijuana groves being discovered as far north as the Upper Peninsula in Michigan. OHRVs provide easier access to these remote locations and present detection problems for the Forest Service as well as the Border Patrol and Customs & Border Protection agents. Many times these DTO are heavily armed and can present not only a danger to law enforcement but also the unsuspecting public who could be recreating in the area.

The expanded use of OHRVs is already negatively affecting both public and private lands. I will cite my home state of New Hampshire where OHRV regulations are principally enforced by the Conservation Officers of the New Hampshire Fish and Game Department. Despite the requirement for successful completion of the mandatory OHRV course, the number of OHRV fatalities has steadily increased. In some areas of the state, Conservation Officers spend over 50 percent of their time enforcing OHRV regulations at the detriment of fish and wildlife protection.

There is no reason to believe that these problems would not be the same on Forest Service and other national lands.

With the scarce funds available for the Forest & National Park Service's legislatively mandated law enforcement programs, both agencies struggle to accommodate the public's needs while protecting the natural resources they are entrusted with. Congress needs to look at better funding the land management agencies so they can effectively manage their programs while protecting the visiting public and the natural resources for everyone to enjoy.

On another issue entirely, there are some who question the Forest Service and other land management agencies exceeding their authority, and question the need for appropriate arms and equipment. This same argument was fought in the Congress before through the Fear of Over-Criminalization and Unjust Seizures legislation, also known as the FOCUS Act. Embedded in the legislation was an attempt to disarm the two agencies that principally enforce the Lacey Act, that being the U.S. Fish & Wildlife & NOAA Fisheries Service's Offices of Law Enforcement. On behalf of FLEOA's FWS and NOAA members, we introduced documents in the Congressional Record justifying the need for these agents being armed. This critical truth remains. Removing criminal law from public land regulation enforcement will cripple the good guys in the fight to keep visitors safe, and our greatest national treasures accessible to all.

In 1984, the U.S. Fish & Wildlife Service, Law Enforcement Division sanctioned and published a study on the Assault Rate on Conservation Law Enforcement Officers in the United States. The study was supported by the Federal Bureau of Investigation as part of their Uniformed Crimes Statistics Program and completed under the direction of then Fish & Wildlife Chief of Law Enforcement, Clark Bavin. Since then the study has been updated several times with the National Park Service annually publishing assault rates on their Law Enforcement Park Rangers.

Non-traditional law enforcement officers in the state and Federal Government were nine times more likely to be assaulted with a dangerous weapon then traditional police officers, who focus primarily is on the enforcement of laws and regulations involving the protection of life and property.

The study suggested that the assault rate could be tied to state and Federal non-traditional law enforcement officers having contact with recreational hunters and commercial and recreational fishers who possess firearms and edged tools and knives. This is complicated by other factors including felons in possession of a firearm while hunting, people homesteading in remote locations on national lands and DTO on public lands and the high seas.

In Federal law enforcement, the National Park Service Law Enforcement Rangers continue to have one of the highest assault rates amongst the 65 Federal law enforcement agencies represented by FLEOA.

These statistics in part lead to increased specialized training for non-traditional law enforcement agencies who have to play a duel role when interacting with the recreating public. They must be Ambassadors who are expected to always be friendly and courteous while maintaining a professional image and demeanor.

Many times news accounts paint non-traditional law enforcement officers as being over-dressed and armed with heavy weaponry while executing arrests or search warrants. It is a reality in today's society that ALL law enforcement officers receive standardized training in areas such as the use of firearms and defensive training. Standardized training is also cost effective as many Federal law enforcement agencies don't have the manpower or material resources to carry out their missions.

There are instances in high-risk situations where non-traditional law enforcement officers may carry automatic weapons and employ other specialized tools that they normally would not carry in the performance of their duties. This also includes the wearing of agency issued raid jackets and clothing for identification purposes and officer safety concerns. This is not only done for liability reasons but for when agencies create task forces or conduct inter-agency operations. Sharing of assets is essential to the efficiency and effectiveness of many smaller Federal law enforcement agencies.

Two examples of how dangerous non-traditional law enforcement can be are:

On March 12, 2014, Forest Service Officer Jason Crisp and his K-9 Maros were ambushed and killed by a double murder suspect hiding in the Pisgah National Forest in Burke County, North Carolina. Officer Crisp had served with the U.S. Forest Service for 16 years. He is survived by his wife and two children, his parents, sister, and two brothers.

Read more about Officer Crisp and Maros at: http://www.odmp.org/officer/22038-officer-jason-m-crisp#ixzz3gr1pKDSy

On January 1, 2012, National Park Service Park Law Enforcement Ranger Margaret Anderson was shot and killed while attempting to stop a fleeing suspect near the Longmire Ranger Station in Mount Rainier National Park, in Pierce County, Washington.

Another park ranger had attempted to stop the suspect at a snow-chain checkpoint near the Paradise Ranger Station, but the suspect fled before being intercepted by Ranger Anderson, who had set up a roadblock. Unbeknownst to Ranger Anderson, the suspect was wanted in connection to a shooting the previous day where four people were wounded. When the suspect reached Ranger Anderson's roadblock, he made a U-turn, exited his vehicle, and opened fire. Ranger Anderson was shot before she was able to exit her patrol car.

After being shot, Ranger Anderson radioed for help as the suspect fled on foot. Responding units attempting to reach Ranger Anderson were held at bay for approximately 90 minutes as the suspect continued to fire on them. The suspect's vehicle was recovered with additional weapons and body armor inside. The suspect's body was found the following day about 6 miles from the initial shooting scene.

Ranger Anderson had served with the National Park Service for 12 years. She is survived by her husband and two young children. Her husband also serves as a park ranger in the park and was on duty at the time. Read more about Ranger Anderson at: http://www.odmp.org/officer/21076-park-ranger-margaret-a-anderson#ixzz3gr35BZqE

In conclusion, the Federal agencies called into question are not here and cannot discuss their perspectives on our conversations today. Before passing judgment on this and the myriad of other issues related to their protocols and perceived conduct, I encourage anyone to consider spending more time with the thousands of state and local authorities that have a productive and effective working relationship with Federal conservation law enforcement. What I strongly discourage is the furtherance of unfounded emotions or baseless theories that only serve to embroider and amplify those who only seek to diminish Federal authority.

There are people out there that refuse to believe that the Earth revolves around the Sun, and because of this simplistic belief, they are willing to exchange an authority controlled by the American people for one of their own, or none at all. This kind of personal conviction is a contagion that does not serve the American people well, and it does even less to preserve public places that are accessible and enjoyable to the average visitor and family.

Federal authority is ultimately an expression of the will of the people and in the case of conservation law enforcement, it is intended to preserve and keep public lands accessible to everyone, not just a few for personal gain. This is not to say that the Federal Government is insensitive to the hardships of local economies. There are plenty of assistance programs to prove it is very helpful in this regard. The Federal agencies work diligently to formulate and respect relationships with state and local entities, and they rely on them heavily for back up and joint rescue and law enforcement operations. This is a time-honored tradition that will never change.

Last, earlier in this testimony I cited only two of many law enforcement officers who were killed in the line of duty protecting our nation's lands and its visitors. While it may be politically popular or advantageous to show law enforcement in a negative light, every time this occurs it adds fuel to an unjustified fire that leads society's weakest minds down a dangerous path. These weak minds identify with messages of false-tyranny and other hateful rhetoric and it provokes them to assault or kill officers for no more reason that what they chose to do as a profession—helping their community and their country. Ambushes against law enforcement officers are growing in this country, as are assaults and other deadly encounters because of the uniform they wear or their lawful duties. In this country, we have a history of shameful treatment against our military women and men during the 1960s and 1970s. Eventually we learned our lesson and now would not think of treating them that way again. We are embarking on the same journey with law enforcement. Must we always learn the hard way? Why do the women and men who serve their communities and their country have to pay for it with their lives? I think there is a better way.

Mr. Chairman, this concludes my testimony at this time and I would be happy to take questions from the Subcommittee on Oversight and Investigations. Thank you for your time and consideration.

———

QUESTIONS SUBMITTED FOR THE RECORD BY DEBBIE DINGELL TO CHRIS SCHOPPMEYER, VICE PRESIDENT FOR AGENCY AFFAIRS, FEDERAL LAW ENFORCEMENT OFFICERS ASSOCIATION

Question 1. How are the majority of agency investigations and cases pursued or prosecuted (civil versus criminal)?

Answer. It depends on the agency. The Interior agencies (FWS, BLM, NPS, BOR & BIA) use the Central Violations Bureau (CVB) for petty offenses, similar to a traffic ticket or summons from a traditional police agency. These CVB tickets can be issued by uniformed officers or special agents of the DOI agencies. For more complex long-term investigations, agencies such as the FWS and their special agents will use the criminal system and have the cases prosecuted by 1 of the 92 DOJ U.S. Attorney's Office. The Dept. of Agriculture's Forest Service handles their cases and investigations similar to the DOI, a combination of petty offense summons through the CVB system while more complex investigations are prosecuted by the DOJ U.S. Attorney's Office. For the Environmental Protection Agency (EPA) they use a combination of civil and criminal remedies for their cases and investigations.

Question 2. Describe the relationship between agencies and the U.S. Attorney's Office related to prosecutions and investigations. How closely do agencies and the AUSA work together?

Answer. In the majority of the 92 DOJ judicial districts, where they deal with environmental and natural resources investigations, the relationship is excellent. Where there may be issues it usually is related to a personality conflict between the uniformed officer or special agent and the prosecuting Assistant U.S. Attorney (AUSA).

Question 3. Can any sheriff do the job of a Forest Service law enforcement officer or agent as Sheriff Brown suggested in the hearing when he said we should reduce Forest Service officers and give sheriffs the savings because they can better respond to and investigate criminal activity?

Answer. The simple answer is no. Deputy Sheriffs are the county law enforcement officers and are trained as traditional police officers, with their principal focus being on protection of life and property. They are not trained in environmental and natural resource law enforcement techniques and investigations. I believe that Sheriff Brown is concerned more with his revenue stream than protecting natural resources. The decrease in revenues received from timber sales on National Forest lands is impacting his operating budget and by decreasing the number of Forest Service law enforcement officers and assuming their jurisdictional role, he stands to increase his budget. That is not just my opinion, it is shared by the majority of our Forest Service members. The question to ask Sheriff Brown is what plan does he have in place to assume the Forest Service law enforcement role and protect the natural resources on Forest Service lands. Deputy Sheriffs will have vast geographic areas to cover with no additional personnel, resources or plan in place.

Question 4. Do you members see themselves primarily as law enforcement officers, caretakers of Federal assets or conservationists?

Answer. Forest Service uniformed officers see themselves as a combination of all three. As I testified during the hearing, "These statistics in part lead to increased specialized training for non-traditional law enforcement agencies who have to play a duel role when interacting with the recreating public. They must be Ambassadors who are expected to always be friendly and courteous while maintaining a professional image and demeanor."

Question 5. For those law enforcement officers and agents supervised by civilians, do they think that is a suitable and safe arrangement?

Answer. You are referring to a management style employed already by the National Park Service. The NPS has over 450 sites which are managed by Superintendents. This style of management can be effective for the law enforcement program as long as the Superintendent supports the law enforcement program. What you refer to in Congress and by the other three witnesses during the hearing as "Stove piping" is actually known as "Line Authority". Line authority is structured so the chain of command is entirely within the law enforcement ranks from uniformed officer or special agent up to the Chief or Director of Law Enforcement. The upper management levels above the Chief or Director of Law Enforcement are typically non-law enforcement managers. Line authority can be more effective as long as you have strong leaders in the law enforcement leadership positions.

Question 6. How have law enforcement programs within Federal agencies reacted to budget cuts over the last few years?

Answer. All 65 Federal law enforcement agencies have been radically impacted by Federal budget cuts since 2008. From the threat of Sequestration to current day, Congress has done a miserable job funding Federal law enforcement programs. The number of unfunded mandates has put Federal law enforcement agencies in a various tenuous position, where less dollars are spread out over more programs in order to meet the mission responsibilities. It has affected the morale in every agency, with many Federal law enforcement officers leaving Federal service for more lucrative and higher paying positions in the private sector.

Question 7. Describe, in general terms, the relationships between Federal law enforcement agencies and state and local law enforcement and other entities? Please focus on coordination and cooperation of operations and enforcement.

Answer. Relationships between Federal law enforcement agencies and their state, county and local counterparts largely depend on individuals and geographic locations. In the eastern part of the United States, relations are generally very cooperative. This may be in part due to there being less land locked up by the Federal Government's land management agencies. For instance in the eastern region of the United States, there are virtually no public lands managed by the BLM. Out in the western United States, lands managed by BLM for grazing have been the source of much contention. One only has to look at the Cliven Bundy situation to see the source of consternation. Bundy refuses to pay his grazing fees on Federal lands while other ranchers complain that they have been paying grazing fees for years and threaten to stop paying the grazing fees unless Cliven Bundy comes into compliance. Before Congress takes a position with regards to Federal relationships out West, you should hold a second hearing and invite a Sheriff from the eastern half of the United States where Federal lands occupy a large percentage of their county. I would seek out a Sheriff from a county in the Green Mountains National Forest in Vermont or the White Mountains National Forest in New Hampshire. I'm sure after they testify Congress will have an entirely different perspective on this issue.

Question 8. How does it affect law enforcement officers in Federal agencies when Members of Congress introduce bills or amendments, or vote for bills or amendments that undermine what they do? How does it affect them when they hear incendiary rhetoric from lawmakers?

Answer. It not only affects morale but it is a multi-faceted issue. Continual budget cuts, lack of staffing and equipment resources are all contributing to the larger issue of employee retention. Congress is quick to criticize how Federal law enforcement agencies conduct business but fail to find real solutions to problems. FLEOA members generally feel that Congress is more about pomp & circumstance than drilling deep into issues and solving problems. An example of this is the aftermath of the Michael Brown shooting involving Police Officer Daryn Wilson. Although Congress' intentions were good in proposing expanded use of body cameras, they failed to provide oversight on how the program would be administered. The DOJ, Bureau of Justice Assistance, responsible for administering the expanded body worn camera program, recommended a grant program for the state, county and local governments, failing to recognize the uniformed components of the Federal law enforcement agencies such as CBP, Border Patrol, and all the land management agencies. Congress needs to do a better job in assisting Federal law enforcement agencies with funding and other priorities and not be so quick to criticize or introduce legislation without adequately investigating the issues at hand.

Mr. GOHMERT. Thank you.

I will now hear from Mr. Larkin. You are recognized for 5 minutes to testify, sir.

Thank you.

STATEMENT OF PAUL LARKIN, JR., SENIOR LEGAL RESEARCH FELLOW, EDWIN MEESE III CENTER FOR LEGAL AND JUSTICE STUDIES, THE HERITAGE FOUNDATION, WASHINGTON, DC

Mr. LARKIN. Thank you, Mr. Chairman, Madam Ranking Member, and other members of the subcommittee.

I am a 1980 graduate of the Stanford Law School and have spent the bulk of my legal career involved in the criminal justice system in one capacity or another. Among the positions I have held are the following: an attorney in the Organized Crime and Racketeering Section of the Criminal Division at the U.S. Justice Department; Assistant to the Solicitor General in the Office of the Solicitor General at the Justice Department; counsel to the Senate Judiciary Committee when it was under the Chairmanship of Senator Orrin Hatch; and Special Agent in Charge in the EPA Criminal Investigation Division.

I have also written on some of the subjects that this committee will address today and perhaps in the future.

I would like to make just a few brief points today. First, it is generally a mistake to use the criminal law for regulatory enforcement. For most of Anglo-American legal history, society has used the criminal law to punish crimes that violated local, cultural mores or norms. The result was that everyone in the community knew what was a crime.

Unfortunately, that is not always the case anymore. Over the last 150 years, American law has started to use the criminal process as an enforcement mechanism in the administrative agencies' enforcement of regulatory programs. While there is no problem with doing that through an administrative or civil process, there is a problem created when you try to use the criminal process.

The problem is, it can be extraordinarily difficult for people to know exactly where the line is between what is permitted and what is prohibited; and the result is you can have the same problems that arise from an unduly vague statute, namely, the average member of the public may not know exactly what is and is not a crime.

Second, even if Congress wants to use law enforcement to enforce regulatory regimes, the job will be better handled, I believe, by traditional law enforcement agencies, such as the Federal Bureau of Investigation and the U.S. Marshal Service.

The public is fully aware of those agencies, but the public, however, is oftentimes completely unaware of other more specialized law enforcement agencies, like those you see at particular regulatory agencies. The result is likely to lead to mistakes of identity, as well as perhaps the sort of problem you talked about, Mr. Chairman, in the overuse of Federal authority.

But equally important is that it runs the risk that regulatory agencies will use their law enforcement agencies on trivial cases in order simply to justify their budget and their existence. That is a problem throughout law enforcement generally. It is not limited just to these agencies, but it has perhaps become most acute when it is.

Third, overuse of SWAT teams and dynamic entries and the like has led to unfortunate results. Witness what happened when county officers made a dynamic entry into the home of the Berwyn Heights, Maryland mayor who was mistakenly suspected to be a drug trafficker. The officers shot and killed his two Labrador Retrievers and terrorized him and his family.

Different Federal agencies with regulatory responsibility have sought this sort of authority as well, and giving it to them, I think, is only likely to lead to more of these sorts of problems.

Given that—I think it was the Ranking Member who mentioned the Lacey Act—let me add just one last point and then I will give my remaining time to you. The Lacey Act raises a host of constitutional problems because of the way it is drafted. What the Lacey Act does is grant Federal lawmaking authority to foreign officials, people who are neither legally nor politically accountable to the public or by the courts.

The result is that the Lacey Act, for those reasons, violates Articles I and II of the Constitution as well as the due process clause.

I have explained this at length in an article that was recently published by the *Harvard Journal of Law and Public Policy*. I have a copy with me, and if you would like, I would be glad to give it to you for submission into the record.

With that, Mr. Chairman, Madam Ranking Member, I give you back my remaining time. I'm glad to answer any questions you have.

[The prepared statement of Mr. Larkin follows:]

PREPARED STATEMENT OF PAUL J. LARKIN, JR., SENIOR LEGAL RESEARCH FELLOW, THE HERITAGE FOUNDATION

Mr. Chairman, Mr. Ranking Member, members of the subcommittee, my name is Paul J. Larkin, Jr. I am a Senior Legal Research Fellow at The Heritage Foundation. The views I express in this testimony are my own and should not be construed as representing any official position of The Heritage Foundation.[1]

Thank you for the opportunity to testify about law enforcement issues that arise in connection with the Federal land management agencies. I have written on some of the issues relevant to the Committee's hearing,[2] and I will draw on those publications for this testimony. I will address three issues identified in the headings below.

[1] The title and affiliation are for identification purposes. Members of The Heritage Foundation staff testify as individuals discussing their own independent research. The views expressed here are my own, and do not reflect an institutional position for The Heritage Foundation or its board of trustees, and do not reflect support or opposition for any specific legislation. The Heritage Foundation is a public policy, research, and educational organization recognized as exempt under section 501(c)(3) of the Internal Revenue Code. It is privately supported and receives no funds from any government at any level, nor does it perform any government or other contract work. The Heritage Foundation is the most broadly supported think tank in the United States. During 2013, it had nearly 600,000 individual, foundation, and corporate supporters representing every state in the U.S. Its 2013 income came from the following sources: 80% from individuals, 17% from foundations, and 3% from corporations. The top five corporate givers provided The Heritage Foundation with 2% of its 2013 income. The Heritage Foundation's books are audited annually by the national accounting firm of McGladrey, LLP.

[2] *See, e.g.,* Paul J. Larkin, Jr., *The Dynamic Incorporation of Foreign Law, and the Constitutional Regulation of Federal Lawmaking*, 38 Harv. J.L. & Pub. Pol'y 337 (2015) (hereafter Larkin, *Dynamic Incorporation*); Paul J. Larkin, Jr., *Strict Liability Offenses, Incarceration, and the Cruel and Unusual Punishments Clause*, 37 Harv. J.L. & Pub. Pol'y 1065 (2014) (hereafter Larkin, *Strict Liability*); Paul J. Larkin, Jr., *Prohibition, Regulation, and Overcriminalization: The Proper and Improper Uses of the Criminal Law*, 42 Hofstra L. Rev. 745 (2014) (hereafter Larkin, *Prohibition, Regulation, and Overcriminalization*); Paul J. Larkin, Jr.,

I. The Problem of Using the Criminal Law for Regulatory and Nontraditional Crimes

A. THE DIFFERENCES BETWEEN COMMON LAW CRIMES AND REGULATORY OR
NONTRADITIONAL CRIMES

1. Using the Criminal Law to Enforce Regulatory Schemes

The threshold question is whether it is sensible to use the criminal law to enforce a regulatory program. In my opinion, the answer is "No" unless there are special circumstances present. The reason why is that the two enforcement schemes differ in several important ways that make any attempt to marry the two likely to fail in most cases. Resorting to criminal law to enforce regulatory programs poses numerous problems not present in the case of traditional "blue-collar" offenses or even standard "white-collar" crimes. Those problems stem from several defining features of regulatory laws that increase the difficulty placed on an average person to understand precisely where the line is drawn between lawful and illegal conduct.

The criminal law prohibits conduct in order for civil society to exist and avoid *bellum omnium contra omnes*.[3] By and large the criminal code addresses the moral code that every person knows by heart and that the private components of a civil society—families, friends, neighbors, members of religious or social organizations, and so forth—teach the young to incorporate into their everyday behavior. By contrast, contemporary regulatory schemes have a very different history and purpose. Regulatory programs grew up, largely in the twentieth century and seek to efficiently manage industries and activities via regulations, policy statements, civil rules, rewards, and penalties to incentivize desirable behavior without casting aspersions on violations attributable to ignorance or explanations other than defiance. Statutes creating those regulatory schemes define the circumstances in which regulated conduct may and may not be undertaken, delegate authority to agencies to promulgate regulations filling out statutory terms, establish permitting and monitoring protocols to ensure that the amount and type of regulated activity does not exceed tolerable limits. Almost without exception, regulatory programs authorize administrative agencies to pursue enforcement through civil processes, not criminal.[4]

The distinction between the civil and criminal laws is an ancient one, with state-administered punishment traditionally reserved only for a violation of the latter.[5] Yet, today many contemporary regulatory programs define unlawful conduct not just as a civil wrong, but also as a crime, and empower the government to penalize regulatory infractions through the same criminal process historically used to investigate, prosecute, and imprison parties for murder, rape, robbery, theft, and a host of other offenses known today as "street" crimes or "blue-collar" crimes. In fact, regulatory criminal laws have become a settled feature of modern-day statutory codes, and they often impose criminal liability for a host of actions that historically would have been considered only civil infractions.

2. Using the Criminal Law to Create Nontraditional Crimes

The second category of problematic uses of the criminal law is in the case of what I will call "nontraditional crimes." I would use the term "traditional crimes" to refer to three subsets of offenses: (a) the crimes that existed at common law—such as murder, rape, robbery, and the like, (b) the similar offenses that contemporary society has added to that list—such as kidnapping, child abuse, peonage, and so forth, and (c) and the crimes that everyone knows are part of today's penal codes, but are not strictly analogous to the type of violent offenses or "street crimes" that that would fit into the two subsets just noted—such as trafficking in controlled substances like heroin. The offenses in this category could overlap with the category of regulatory crimes discussed above, because agency rules may define relevant terms or set limits to the amount and type of such conduct that may permissibly be done. But some nontraditional crimes will be defined by statute without the

---

Taking Mistakes Seriously, 28 B.Y.U. J. of Pub. L. 71 (2014); Paul J. Larkin, Jr., *Public Choice Theory and Overcriminalization*, 36 Harv. J.L. & Pub. Pol'y 715 (2013) (hereafter Larkin, *Overcriminalization*); Paul J. Larkin, Jr., *A Mistake of Law Defense as a Remedy for Overcriminalization*, 26 A.B.A.J. Criminal Justice 10 (Spring 2013).

[3] *See* Thomas Hobbes, Leviathan 80 (1651).

[4] *See* Max Minzner, *Why Agencies Punish*, 53 Wm. & Mary L. Rev. 853, 858–59 (2012).

[5] *See* Jerome Hall, *Interrelations of Criminal Law and Torts*, 43 Colum. L. Rev. 753, 757–58 (1943).

assistance of supporting regulations.[6] The common denominator for crimes that fit into this category is that they address conduct that is not always unlawful.

B. THE IMPORTANCE OF THOSE DIFFERENCES

Resorting to criminal law to enforce regulatory programs poses numerous, difficult compliance problems not present in the case of traditional "blue-collar" offenses or even standard "white-collar" crimes. Those problems stem from several defining features of regulatory laws that increase the difficulty placed on an average person to understand precisely where the line is drawn between lawful and illegal conduct. Treating regulatory crimes as if they were no different than "street crimes" ignores the profound difference between the two classes of offenses and puts parties engaged in entirely legitimate activities without any intent to break the law at risk of criminal punishment. In fact, many of the features that make the administrative process a desirable, and sometimes necessary, means for implementing acts of Congress render inappropriate use of the criminal process as an enforcement mechanism.

Consider this example. Congress may, and often does, use a broadly defined term (for example, "solid waste") in a statute (for example, the Resource Conservation and Recovery Act) that delegates to an agency (for example, the EPA) the power to implement that law by elaborating or refining the definition of a term (for example, "hazardous waste"), by creating a list of specific examples of what that term means (for example, "listed hazardous wastes"), or by specifying exemptions from the term (for example, "recyclable materials").[7] By legislating in that fashion, Congress can grant the executive branch considerable regulatory flexibility. An agency can adapt existing regulations or promulgate new ones whenever necessary to address worsening or newly emerging hazards without having to return to Congress for specific supplemental regulatory authorization. That practice also enables the agency to invoke its superior technical and scientific expertise regarding a particular substance, production process, or medical risk whenever a new problem pops up or an old one takes a turn for the worse. Broadly written regulatory statutes granting administrative agencies room to maneuver are valuable because society wants agencies to be able to respond quickly (for instance) to serious health threats by revising the rules necessary to forestall or remedy a problem. At the same time, the freedom to respond quickly can place individuals at risk of criminal punishment for guessing mistakenly about what the law requires because regulatory developments can outpace their knowledge of the law.

The evolving nature of regulations, however, is only one aspect of the notice problem. An elementary principle of criminal and constitutional law is that the government must clearly identify particular conduct as criminal so that the average person, without resort to legal advice, can comply with the law.[8] Historically, that requirement posed little difficulty. The government ordinarily could satisfy that obligation simply by enacting and making public a statute that was written in terms the average person could readily understand. Throughout Anglo-American legal history, contemporary mores condemned certain conduct as harmful, dangerous, or blameworthy, such as murder, rape, robbery, and burglary.[9] A legislature could readily draft a straightforward, easily comprehensible ordinance outlawing those actions by drawing on language widely understood in the community. That is not the case, however, in fields that are subject to regulation or that criminalize nontraditional conduct.

Start with the quantity of relevant laws. The total number of Federal statutes and regulations relevant to criminal conduct is unknown but likely is immense.[10] Some commentators have estimated that there are more than 4,450 Federal criminal statutes and more than 300,000 Federal regulations that define conduct as criminal or otherwise bear on the proper interpretation of the laws that do.[11] No one—no

---

[6] The Computer Fraud and Abuse Act (CFAA), 18 U.S.C. § 1030 (2012), is an example. It prohibits only certain uses of computers and does not delegate authority to an administrative agency to define precisely what uses are impermissible. *See generally* Paul J. Larkin, Jr., *United States v. Nosal: Rebooting the Computer Fraud and Abuse Act*, 8 Seton Hall Cir. Rev. 257, 260–261 & nn. 11–13 (2012) (collecting authorities interpreting the CFAA).

[7] *See* Larkin, *Strict Liability, supra* note 1, at 1088–89.

[8] *See, e.g.*, Rogers v. Tennessee, 532 U.S. 451, 459 (2001).

[9] *See, e.g.*, Livingston Hall & Selig J. Seligman, *Mistake of Law and Mens Rea*, 8 U. Chi. L. Rev. 641, 644 (1941) ("[T]he early criminal law appears to have been well integrated with the mores of the time, out of which it arose as 'custom.'"); Larkin, *Dynamic Incorporation, supra* note 1, at 382 (collecting authorities).

[10] *See* Michael B. Mukasey & Paul J. Larkin, Jr., *The Perils of Overcriminalization*, The Heritage Foundation, Legal Memorandum No. 146, at 1–2 & nn. 6–7 (Feb. 12, 2015), http://thf_media.s3.amazonaws.com/2015/pdf/LM146.pdf; *see id.* at 1–2 nn. 6–8.

[11] *See id.*

lawyer, no judge, no law professor—has that knowledge. As the distinguished academic and late Harvard Law School professor William Stuntz put it: "Ordinary people do not have the time or training to learn the contents of criminal codes; indeed, even criminal law professors rarely know much about what conduct is and isn't criminal in their jurisdictions."[12] Permitting the government to rest criminal liability on the fiction that the average person is conversant with the ins and outs of Federal regulatory statutes, let alone the thousands of potentially relevant regulations, borders on the obscene.

If it is unreasonable to expect that everyone already knows the law, people must be able to find it. Yet, even finding every pertinent regulation can be an onerous task. Few people are aficionados of the U.S. Code, let alone the Code of Federal Regulations or the Federal Register. Given the massive increase in the number of Federal regulations over the last century, there is a potentially enormous number of ways that someone can violate criminal statutes today. The result makes it almost certain that the average person will be completely unaware of some of those ways that he or she can break the law.

There is an additional complicating factor. Federal Government officials responsible for implementing domestic statutory programs often construe relevant acts of Congress and agency regulations in publicly issued "guidance documents" or "compliance manuals," as well as in internal memoranda.[13] Interpretations that have not been promulgated as regulations do not have the same legal status as agency rules, of course, but they still may have considerable legal effect. An agency's construction of its own regulations is generally deemed controlling on the courts unless that interpretation is unconstitutional or contrary to the plain text of the rule itself.[14] An agency's interpretive memoranda that are not publicly available are tantamount to a form of "secret" or "underground" law.[15]

Even if the average person can find all of the pertinent regulations and internal agency guidance documents, however, there is no guarantee that he or she can *understand* them, given the often-recondite rules that agencies adopt for subjects that are technical or scientific in nature. The relevant statutes vest broad authority and discretion in the expert agencies in order to permit them the flexibility deemed necessary for them to respond to advances in scientific and medical knowledge and changes in manufacturing or other productive mechanisms. Regulations promulgated by agencies can form highly reticulated networks demanding a sophisticated understanding of technical subjects beyond the ken of the average person.[16] The result often is that agency rules, such as the ones promulgated under the Federal environmental laws, can be extraordinarily abstruse, demanding almost as much scientific or technical knowledge as legal skill to ensure their proper interpretation.[17] Yet, fair notice of what the law forbids is a longstanding requirement for imposing criminal punishment. It is settled law that the government cannot criminally enforce a law that cannot be understood by a person "of ordinary intelligence."[18] A technical set of rules thus can create the same notice problems that we already acknowledge to exist when a statute is unduly vague. In both cases the average person would not know what has been made a crime. Just as the criminal law does not require a person to consult with an attorney in order to avoid liability, so, too, it should not demand that an individual resort to a biologist, geologist, or hydrologist before undertaking facially reasonable activity in a legitimate business.

Another complicating factor with regulatory or nontraditional crimes is that their prohibitions may not apply across the board. Murder is always a crime; the criminal law prohibits every instance of this conduct, not merely the ones that exceed a defined limit. Every rape is a crime; other factors may aggravate that offense, but the basic crime exists in every criminal code. Robbery fits into the same category; no one can apply for a permit to commit robberies. By contrast, not every use of a computer is a Federal offense, the disposal of household garbage is not the same as the dumping of hazardous waste, and a party can apply for a permit to pollute the nation's waterways.

The raison d'être of a regulatory program is that certain conduct cannot or should not be forbidden in all circumstances and so must be managed, controlled, or supervised to limit the instances in which it occurs or poses a hazard. A statute may

---

[12] William J. Stuntz, *Self-Defeating Crimes*, 86 Va. L. Rev. 1871, 1871 (2000).

[13] *See, e.g.*, Larkin, *Dynamic Incorporation, supra* note 1, at 384.

[14] *See* Auer v. Robbins, 519 U.S. 452, 461–62 (1997).

[15] *See* Kathleen F. Brickey, *Environmental Crime at the Crossroads: The Intersection of Environmental and Criminal Law Theory*, 71 Tul. L. Rev. 487, 502–03 (1996).

[16] *See* Larkin, *Strict Liability, supra* note 1, at 1092–93.

[17] For a good example, see Vidrine v. United States, 846 F. Supp. 2d 550, 561–69 (W.D. La. 2011) (involving the issue whether used oil was a recyclable product or hazardous waste).

[18] United States v. Harriss, 347 U.S. 612, 617 (1954).

empower an agency to issue a permit to conduct certain activity, and the agency's rules may define when, where, how, and by whom that conduct may be done. But it is more difficult to comply with a carefully nuanced rule than with a diktat forbidding any and all instances of identified conduct. Even the lawyers who practice in a regulated industry may not know all of the statutes, rules, regulations, and agency interpretations—which makes hopeless the plight of the average person who lacks legal training, or ready and inexpensive access to an attorney.[19] The result is that it can be difficult for the average person to know when he or she has crossed over the line into forbidden territory.[20]

Historically, mens rea requirements have mediated between the need for flexibility and the duty to notify the public what the law forbids by limiting criminal liability to someone who intentionally violates a known legal duty or commits easily recognizable blameworthy conduct. At common law, a crime consisted of "a vicious will" and "an unlawful act consequent upon such vicious will."[21] That principle still has resonance today.[22] The criminal law traditionally has looked askance on negligence as a basis for liability and has treated strict liability crimes with outright scorn.[23]

Regulatory programs, however, often do not treat scienter with the same respect.[24] The reason for that slight is that regulatory laws see their goal as protection of the public against particular insults or hazards, such as carcinogens, that cause insidious short- or long-term harm regardless of the intent or knowledge of the party responsible for their creation or misuse.[25] Public health programs, for example, seek to empower agencies such as the Food and Drug Administration or the Environmental Protection Agency to intervene in the manufacturing, distribution, or disposal processes in order to prevent adulterated drugs from entering the stream of commerce, or to keep hazardous waste from poisoning the water supply, regardless of whether the party involved was aware of or oblivious to the dangers that his conduct posed.[26] Injunctive remedies are reasonable devices for preventing public injury, and after-the-fact civil or administrative fines serve reasonable educative and deterrent purposes.[27] But the criminal law is society's most powerful weapon against conduct deemed unlawful and traditionally has been brought to bear on an individual only when he acted with a wicked intent, rather than merely negligently, let alone when no blame at all can be attributed to him. Regulatory laws do not see it that way. That creates serious notice and compliance problem for small businesses and individuals.

II. The Multiplication of Federal Law Enforcement Agencies

Most Americans have heard of a small number of Federal law enforcement agencies, such as the Federal Bureau of Investigation (FBI), the Drug Enforcement Administration (DEA), the Secret Service, the U.S. Marshal's Service, and perhaps one or two others. What they do not know is that there is "a dizzying array" of other Federal investigative agencies,[28] more than 100 of them. The total number of agents

---

[19] See Edwin Meese III & Paul J. Larkin, Jr., *Reconsidering the Mistake of Law Defense*, 102 J. Crim. L. & Criminology 725, 742–43 (2012).

[20] See United States v. McNab, 331 F.3d 1228 (11th Cir. 2003) (defendant sentenced to 8 years in prison for importing undersized, egg-bearing lobsters from Honduras in violation of Honduran law). In the Gibson Guitar case, the Department of Justice investigated Gibson Guitar for a violation of the laws of Madagascar even though at least one of the relevant laws had to be translated into English. *See* Letter Containing a Deferred Prosecution Agreement from Jerry E. Martin, U.S. Attorney, M.D. Tenn., et al., to Donald A. Carr & William M. Sullivan Jr. App. A, at 6 (July 27, 2012) [hereinafter GIBSON GUITAR DPA] (referring to "the Department's translation of Interministerial Order 16.030/2006"), http://www.legaltimes.typepad.com/files/gibson.pdf [http://perma.cc/RQV9-F2WB].

[21] 4 William Blackstone, Commentaries on the Laws of England 21 (1979).

[22] See, e.g., McFadden v. United States, 135 S. Ct. 2298, 2304 (2015); Elonis v. United States, 135 S. Ct. 2001, 2008–10 (2015).

[23] See, e.g., Henry M. Hart, Jr., *The Aims of the Criminal Law*, 23 L. & Contemp. Probs. 401, 421–22 (1958); Larkin, *Strict Liability, supra* note 1, at 1079 n. 46 (collecting authorities).

[24] See Meese & Larkin, *supra* note 20, at 744–45.

[25] *Id.* at 744.

[26] *See id.*

[27] Hudson v. United States, 522 U.S. 93, 102 (1997) ("all civil penalties have some deterrent effect").

[28] Louise Radnofsky, Gary Fields & John R. Emshwiller, *Federal Police Ranks Swell to Enforce a Widening Array of Criminal Laws*, Wall St. J., Dec. 17, 2011, at A1 *available at* http://online.wsj.com/article/SB10001424052970203518404577094861497383678.html#project%3DREG S121520111215%26articleTabs%3Darticle ("For years, the public face of Federal law enforcement has been the Federal Bureau of Investigation. Today, for many people, the knock on the door is increasingly likely to come from a dizzying array of other police forces tucked away

could fill out 10 divisions of armed Federal law enforcement officers. The multiplication of Federal law enforcement agencies can lead to numerous problems.[29]

A. THE NUMBER OF FEDERAL LAW ENFORCEMENT AGENCIES AND OFFICERS

The Bureau of Justice Statistics (BJS), a component of the U.S. Department of Justice, conducted a census in September 2008 of 73 agencies and 33 inspector general's offices. BJS concluded that there were approximately 120,000 full-time Federal law enforcement officers, parties authorized to make arrests and carry firearms in the United States.[30] The bulk of those officers—roughly 45,000 or 37 percent—conducted criminal investigations and enforcement duties. The second largest category consisted of police response and patrol officers—about 28,000 officers or 23 percent of the total. Next came immigration or custom inspection officers—approximately 18,000 in number or 15 percent—followed by officers performing correctional or detention-related duties—about 17,000 or 14 percent.[31]

Putting aside inspector generals' offices, 24 Federal agencies employed 250 or more full-time law enforcement personnel—that is, personnel with arrest and firearms-possession authority—with the four largest agencies fitting into two parent organizations; the Departments of Homeland Security and Justice. The U.S. Customs and Border Protection (CBP) (36,863 full-time officers) and the U.S. Immigration and Customs Enforcement Agency (ICE) (12,446) are components of the Homeland Security Department, while the Federal Bureau of Prisons (BOP) (16,835) and the FBI (12,760) are units within the Justice Department. The Homeland Security Department also contains the U.S. Secret Service (5,213) and the Federal Protective Service (900). The Justice Department also housed the DEA (4,308), the U.S. Marshal's Service (3,313), and the Bureau of Alcohol, Tobacco, Firearms, and Explosives (2,541), three other agencies in the 24 largest Federal law enforcement agencies. In addition, 16 Federal agencies employ fewer than 250 full-time officers.[32] Among them are the Environmental Protection Agency (EPA) and the Food and Drug Agency (FDA).[33]

Several Federal law enforcement agencies appear to be within the Committee's jurisdiction. A few of them are listed among the agencies employing 250 or more full-time law enforcement personnel: the National Park Service Rangers (1,404), the U.S. Forest Service (644), the U.S. Fish & Wildlife Service (598), the National Park Service Park Police (547), the Bureau of Indian Affairs (277), and the Bureau of Land Management (255).[34] Two agencies among those with fewer than 250 full-time officers also appear to fit within the Committee's jurisdiction: the National Oceanic and Atmospheric Administration's (NOAA) National Marine Fisheries Service (149) and the Bureau of Reclamation (21).[35] Finally, the Office of the Inspector General for the Department of the Interior (66) would seem to fit within the Committee's

inside lesser-known crime-fighting agencies. They could be from the Environmental Protection Agency, the Labor or Education Departments, the National Park Service, the Bureau of Land Management or the National Oceanic and Atmospheric Administration, the agency known for its weather forecasts.").

[29] The General Accounting Office and its successor the Government Accountability Office have conducted several studies of the issues posed by numerous Federal law enforcement agencies. *See, e.g.*, Government Accountability Office, Federal Law Enforcement: Survey of Federal Civilian Law Enforcement Functions and Authorities, GAO–07–121 (Dec. 19, 2006), available at http://www.gao.gov/new.items/d07121.pdf; Government Accountability Office, Results of Surveys of Federal Civilian Law Enforcement Components, An E-Supplement To GAO–07–121, GAO–07–223SP (Dec. 19, 2006), available at http://www.gao.gov/special.pubs/gao-07-223sp/index.html; General Accounting Office, Federal Law Enforcement Training Center: Capacity Planning and Management Oversight Need Improvement, GAO–03–736 (July 24, 2003), available at http://www.gao.gov/assets/240/239049.pdf; General Accounting Office, Inspectors General: Comparison of Ways Law Enforcement Authority is Granted, GAO–02–437 (May 22, 2002), available at http://www.gao.gov/assets/240/234071.pdf; General Accounting Office, Federal Law Enforcement: Investigative Authority and Personnel at 32 Organizations, GAO/GGD–97–93 (July 22, 1997), available at http://www.gao.gov/assets/230/224401.pdf; General Accounting Office, Federal Law Enforcement: Investigative Authority and Personnel at 13 Agencies, GAO/GGD–96–154 (Sept. 30, 1996), available at http://www.gao.gov/assets/230/223212.pdf.

[30] *See* U.S. Dep't of Justice, Bureau of Justice Statistics, Federal Law Enforcement, 2008, NCJ 238250, at 1 (June 2012).

[31] *Id.*

[32] *Id.* at 5 Tbl. 2.

[33] *Id.* at 3, 5 Tbl. 2.

[34] *Id.* at 2 Tbl. 1, 4.

[35] *Id.* at 5 & Tbl. 2.

jurisdiction.[36] In sum, there are approximately 3,700 officers under this Committee's oversight jurisdiction.

B. PROBLEMS CREATED BY GRANTING FEDERAL REGULATORY AGENCIES LAW ENFORCEMENT AUTHORITY

Congress could use civil investigative units for Federal agencies and grant them the power to compel private parties to submit to on-site civil inspections.[37] Civil compliance officers, however, lack the authority and respect given to Federal agents. In comparison to civil inspectors, FBI agents wearing "raid jackets" emblazoned with the Bureau's logo will receive far more deference from a judge, a corporation, and the public. To take advantage of the nimbus that law enforcement officers radiate, Congress may create a minor crime (that is, a misdemeanor or minor offense) so that a regulatory agency can call on the full Federal investigative apparatus for inspection purposes, instead of being forced to show up at a plant with hat in hand to negotiate with a corporation's lawyers over the scope of an inspection. Adding criminal statutes to an otherwise entirely civil regulatory scheme allows Congress to cash in on the leverage that a criminal investigation enjoys with the public and the media.[38]

A closely related factor is the growth of specialized Federal investigative agencies. Federal law enforcement agencies differ from state and local police departments with respect to the scope of their authority. As an incidence of a state's "police power," a state can authorize state and local police forces to investigate any and all violations of state law. This is not the case for Federal investigators. Just as the Federal Government is a polity of limited powers, so too, Federal law enforcement agencies have only the authority that Congress grants them. Most people are familiar with agencies, such as the FBI, which has broad investigative authority.[39] The creation of specialized law enforcement agencies, however, raises a problem analogous to one that existed with respect to the independent counsel provisions of the Ethics in Government Act of 1978 [40]: loss of perspective.[41] Agencies with wide-ranging investigative responsibility see the entire range of human conduct and can put any one party's actions into a broad perspective. Agencies with a narrow charter see only what they investigate. If the only tool that one has to use is a hammer, everything looks like a nail. The result is that specialized agencies may wind up pursuing trivial criminal cases to justify their existence and continued Federal funding.[42]

It also is difficult to change a criminal investigation into a civil inquiry midstream. Differences in evidentiary rules, sources of information, and the certainty required to impose sanctions all complicate a hand off between Federal agents and administrators. Crimes committed in regulated industries are generally "white-collar" in nature, which means that Federal investigators need to wade through a sea of documents. The easiest way to get documents from the target of an investigation is by issuing the company a grand jury subpoena because a Federal grand jury

---

[36] *Id.* at 6 Tbl. 3.

[37] *See, e.g.*, the Antitrust Civil Process Act of 1962, Pub. L. No. 87–664, 76 Stat. 548 (codified in various sections of 15 U.S.C. § 1311) (authorizing Justice Department attorneys to issue civil investigative demands to obtain documents from the target of a civil antitrust investigation); New York v. Burger, 482 U.S. 691 (1987) (upholding state law authorizing the warrantless search of the premises of vehicle dismantlers and junkyards).

[38] *See* Gerard E. Lynch, *The Role of Criminal Law in Policing Corporate Misconduct*, 60 Law & Contemp. Probs. 23, 37 (1997). That phenomenon may explain the provenance of the criminal provisions of the Federal environmental laws. Initially, those laws created only misdemeanors. *See* Richard J. Lazarus, *Meeting the Demands of Integration in the Evolution of Environmental Law: Reforming Environmental Criminal Law*, 83 Geo. L. J. 2407, 2446–47 (1995) (footnotes omitted).

[39] The FBI has the broadest authority of any Federal law enforcement agency. The Secret Service and Marshals Service are close behind. *See* Larkin, *Overcriminalization, supra* note 1, at 739 n. 95.

[40] Ethics in Government Act of 1978, Pub. L. No. 95–521, 92 Stat. 1824.

[41] *Cf.* Morrison v. Olson, 487 U.S. 654, 727–32 (1988) (Scalia, J., dissenting).

[42] "Federal prosecutors already operate under an incentive structure that forces them to focus on the statistical 'bottom line.' Statistics on arrests and convictions are the Justice Department's bread and butter. They are submitted to the department's outside auditors, are instrumental in assessing the 'performance' of the U.S. Attorneys' Offices, and are the focus of the department's annual report. As George Washington University Law School professor Jonathan Turley puts it, 'In some ways, the Justice Department continues to operate under the body count approach in Vietnam . . . .. They feel a need to produce a body count to Congress to justify past appropriations and secure future increases.'" Gene Healy, *There Goes the Neighborhood: The Bush-Ashcroft Plan to "Help" Localities Fight Gun Crime*," in Go Directly to Jail: The Criminalization of Almost Everything 105–06 (Gene Healy ed., 2004).

has broad investigative authority and there is little that a firm can do to challenge a subpoena.[43] Once the Federal Government gets its mitts on subpoenaed documents, however, it is extremely difficult for the government to transfer them to civil enforcers.[44] Federal law enforcement officers cannot routinely disclose grand jury materials to their civil colleagues; the government must instead make a showing of "particularized need" for grand jury materials in order to make use of them in a civil proceeding.[45] This difficulty gives the government a strong incentive to maintain as a criminal investigation any inquiry begun as such.

C. PROBLEMS CREATED BY HAVING MULTIPLE FEDERAL LAW ENFORCEMENT AGENCIES

The large number of Federal law enforcement agencies can lead to a variety of problems.

First, the large number of agencies makes it difficult for the public to know whether a particular Federal officer in fact is a Federal agent. The public can readily identify local law enforcement officers. Whether police officers or deputy sheriffs, state and local police officers dress in easily recognizable uniforms, they interact with the public during the course of official business, and they often are friends or neighbors in the community. The public is also familiar with officers performing purely investigative functions, such as "detectives" or "inspectors," because numerous films and television shows have portrayed those officers in action. As far as Federal law enforcement officers go, the public also knows about the FBI, the DEA, the U.S. Marshal's Service, and perhaps one or two others, but is wholly unaware that a vast number of other Federal agencies, such as the EPA, the FDA, and NOAA, also employ agents with criminal investigative authority. To most members of the public, those are purely regulatory agencies with responsibilities that have nothing to do with the criminal law (for NOAA, the public thinks of dolphins) or that are more a source of amusement than respect (for the EPA, the public thinks of Walter Peck in "*Ghostbusters*"). The public's inability easily to identify as legitimate members of the law enforcement community parties claiming to be Federal agents working for nontraditional law enforcement agencies, to my knowledge, has led to dangerous confrontations and, in my view, is certain to ultimately result in an unfortunate incident where one party or the other is shot.

Second, the large number of agencies leads to needless waste. Keep in mind that agents are not the only personnel at a law enforcement agency. The problem with more than 100 Federal law enforcement agencies is that they may be considerable overlap or "slack" in the system that should be alleviated by combining functions. For example, while it is important to have lawyers dedicated to working exclusively with agents, there may be no need for a separate cadre of lawyers at each Federal law enforcement agency. Consolidating agencies could eliminate expenditure on needless resources.

Third, adding criminal divisions to regulatory agencies is hardly a guarantee that regulatory crimes will be adequately investigated. That is true for several reasons. To start with, there is no guarantee that the agency will have the necessary resources to investigate crimes. There may be an equal or greater number of ancillary support personnel who perform missions critical to the success of the agency. As far as personnel goes, any agency must have lawyers, evidence collection experts, laboratory technicians, training officers, and administrative personnel in addition to the parties authorized to make arrests and carry firearms. (Of course, some agents also will perform supervisory functions and therefore would not be available for fieldwork.) Agencies must also have offices, vehicles, computers, and other equipment. Moreover, criminal investigation units may not even be welcome in a regulatory agency. They may be seen as a drain on agency resources, as a sop to whatever parties want the relevant conduct to be made a crime, or as a diversion from the agency's primary mission of pursuing the requisite scientific, technical, or economic inquiries necessary to justify promulgating regulations to govern private conduct. Some regulatory agency criminal programs may be little more than Potemkin Villages, units designed to display an interest in criminal enforcement that is not genuine, or serve as the threatened agency component to which a matter will be referred if a party refuses to accept a civil or administrative settlement of a matter.

---

[43] *See* Fed. R. Crim. P. 6, 17(c); United States v. R. Enterprises, Inc., 498 U.S. 292, 297 (1991).
[44] *See* Peter C. Yeager, The Limits of Law: The Public Regulation of Private Pollution 35 (1991).
[45] *See* United States v. Sells Eng'g, Inc., 463 U.S. 418, 443 (1983).

Fourth, the large number of agencies makes congressional oversight difficult, particularly when different congressional committees have jurisdiction over different Federal agencies.

III. The Overmilitarization of Federal Law Enforcement

Media images of tanks and armored personnel carriers in urban streets, heavily armed government agents clad in helmets, BDUs, and other military-style gear, and sharpshooters waiting patiently for "Execute" orders bring to mind images of the Russian Federation's annexation of the Crimea in 2014 or the former Soviet Union's invasions of Hungary in 1956, Czechoslovakia in 1968, and Afghanistan in 1979. Unfortunately, the images also occasionally describe stories about the civil unrest that has periodically rent our society or the unnecessary and unwise use of SWAT units for law enforcement purposes. Traditional Federal law enforcement agencies—the FBI, the Secret Service, the Marshal's Service, for example—have need of SWAT units for the different type of work they do. Entering structures where terrorists are plotting their crimes, where violent criminal are "holed up," or where large quantities of controlled substances are being held for distribution—those and some other instances are classic examples of the need for the specialized training and equipment that SWAT units have. Unfortunately, however, other Federal agencies may also seek to have comparable units of their own. The proliferation of these units can create terrible problems for Federal law enforcement, not the least of which is the increasing perception of the American public that law enforcement officers have taken on the image and attitude of military Special Forces units.

Militarization of law enforcement will inevitably lead to incidents that no one wants to see happen but that everyone, if honest, knows will inevitably occur. Once an agency has a SWAT team, the team will deploy frequently. The team members will want to work in that capacity as often as possible because it is far more fun to break down a door than to review the boxes of papers that are the grist for the mill in a white-collar criminal investigation. The unit's supervisors will want to deploy the team to prove that it is a necessity. But there are only so many heavily fortified biker meth labs, so agency SWAT units will wind up being deployed in settings where there is no good reason for them to be called out—like the incident in which suburban Maryland officers mistakenly made a dynamic entry into the home of the local mayor and shot his two Labrador Retrievers.[46] The result will be needless deaths.

There are a few additional points to keep in mind. *First*, there is likely to be a very small number of instances in which regulatory and nontraditional crimes need the special skills of a SWAT team and only a small number of Federal agencies that need such a unit on call. *Second*, there are several Federal agencies, such as the FBI and Marshal's Service, with officers dedicated to the work done by a SWAT team. A Federal agency that believes a SWAT team is necessary can call on one of those agencies for assistance.[47] *Third*, Federal agencies need to accept the fact that going without your own SWAT team does not make you an inferior law enforcement agency. There is nothing remotely degrading about working in a field that is dedicated to the investigation of white-collar crimes. Keeping your neighbors safe from grifters is a noble undertaking. *Fourth*, despite what Ben Franklin said, we need to make a trade-off between security and freedom. Militarizing Federal law enforcement agencies will engender suspicion, hostility, and resentment, all of which will poison the relationship that the Federal agents need in order to carry out their investigative responsibilities.

Does this mean that there never will be an occasion in which a SWAT team is necessary to enforce a regulatory scheme or a nontraditional crime? Of course not. Whether such a unit is necessary must be answered in each case based on its own facts. After all, violent criminals can commit regulatory or nontraditional crimes. But there are Federal agencies with trained personnel, like the FBI and Marshal's Service, which can assist when such units are necessary.

---

[46] *See, e.g.*, Radley Balko, Rise of the Warrior Cop: The Militarization of America's Police Forces (2014).

[47] In some instances, a Federal regulatory agency also may be able to enlist state or local police officers for assistance. For example, the New York City Police Department has an Emergency Services Unit that functions as a SWAT unit.

Conclusion

Thank you for the opportunity to offer the subcommittee my views on these law enforcement issues. I am glad to answer any questions that members of the subcommittee may have, and I also am willing to help the subcommittee in its work.

*****

The following item was submitted by Mr. Larkin for the record and will be retained in the Committee's official files:

—Article: Public Choice Theory and Overcriminalization. Paul J. Larkin, Jr. *Harvard Journal of Law & Public Policy*, (2013).

———

Mr. GOHMERT. Thank you very much, Mr. Larkin.

We appreciate all of your testimony today. At this time we are going to move into questioning by the Members. I am going to be here for the duration of the hearing, so I am going to recognize first my colleague and my friend from Georgia, Mr. Hice, for 5 minutes for questions.

Dr. HICE. Thank you very much, Mr. Chairman, and I appreciate this hearing to, frankly, examine the accountability of enforcement divisions of the Department of the Interior as well as the U.S. Forest Service.

Before I begin my questions, like a number of other Members here on the subcommittee, my home state of Georgia was directly impacted by the very issue that we are dealing with this morning. Both north Georgia and the western portion of North Carolina were recently the focal point of a 4-year, multi-Federal and state joint operation called "Operation Something Bruin."

I do not know if you are familiar with that, but it involved the Forest Service, Fish and Wildlife Service, Park Service, the Georgia Department of Natural Resources, and the North Carolina Wildlife Resources Commission, and what they were trying to do was to stop a group of individuals who were illegally killing bears in that portion of our country.

"Operation Something Bruin" came to a head in February of 2013 with the prosecution of 51 different individuals on both Federal and state charges. Last month our colleague, Mark Meadows, who is on the Oversight and Government Reform Committee, but chairs within that committee the Government Operations Subcommittee, held a field hearing in Waynesville, North Carolina, on that particular operation and how it transpired. It involved testimony from private citizens as well as Federal and state agencies.

What was found was alarming to me. Media reports as well as individual testimony found that at least three of our agents, undercover officers, actually killed bears during that, and they were actively involved in trying to entrap other hunters in that whole ordeal.

There were also accounts of our Federal raids—our agents federally raiding and seizing personal property, damaging property that was unrelated to the whole ordeal.

I commend Chairman Meadows on that particular operation, and, Chairman, I would like to ask unanimous consent to include letters from Mr. Meadows to the Inspectors General of the

Department of the Interior and Agriculture and those responses in the record if I can, sir.

Mr. GOHMERT. Without objection, so ordered.

Dr. HICE. With that, let me begin, Mr. Larkin, with you. Are you familiar, by the way, with "Operation Something Bruin"?

Mr. LARKIN. I am not as familiar as you are. I have read an article about it; so I am generally familiar with it, but not with the specifics.

Dr. HICE. OK. Based on what I just shared with you about that, it is an extremely, to me at least, elaborate example of Federal agencies working with state officials in this regard. There were a lot of controversies, as I mentioned.

Do you believe this is a wise use of Federal law enforcement resources?

Mr. LARKIN. No, I do not. I think enforcement of the fish and game laws and the like should be left to state and local authorities. Generally speaking, they have the authority even if the property that is at issue is in the concurrent jurisdiction of the Federal and state governments.

If the property happens to be within the exclusive jurisdiction of the Federal Government, then the regulations promulgated by the U.S. Marshal Service allow the Marshal to designate state and local law enforcement officers as Special Deputy U.S. Marshals, so that they can then enforce the state laws in that area.

Now, the problem here is also a more general one. Federal law enforcement agencies have grown up in a haphazard manner over the course of the Nation's history. Originally we started with the Marshal Service and the Customs Service—the Marshal Service because we needed someone like a sheriff; the Customs Service because the only way we made any money was through the taxes imposed on importation and exportation.

All of the other agencies have grown up without Congress ever stepping back and asking itself this question: What are the crimes that only the Federal Government can handle? And there are some.

Only the Federal Government can handle espionage, international terrorism, state and local political corruption, civil rights violations, environmental crimes, interstate complex or very sophisticated fraud. Those are the sorts of crimes that the Federal Government should focus on; and it should limit its assets devoted to law enforcement to those sorts of matters, not the Fish and Game matters.

Dr. HICE. OK, sir. Thank you.

I did have some other questions for the sheriff, but my time has expired. I yield back. Thank you.

Mr. GOHMERT. Thank you.

At this time we will recognize the Ranking Member, Congresswoman Dingell, for 5 minutes.

Mrs. DINGELL. Thank you.

Let me just ask one question following up on that, and then I have some questions for Mr. Schoppmeyer.

From what you just said, are you saying that state and locals should be in charge of law enforcement on Federal lands?

Mr. LARKIN. They should handle the law enforcement crimes that state and local law enforcement officers can handle. It does not mean that we should denude Federal law enforcement officers of all their ability on Federal land.

For example, were a Marshal or were an FBI agent to see a violent crime committed in his or her presence, that agent should step in and handle that; but Federal agents are trained and are qualified to handle crimes that only the Federal Government can. So, whenever you divert their time and their assets and their resources to handle crimes that state and local people can handle, you take away from what they can do.

You see, the problem often in law enforcement is not that there is not a law that deals with the problem. The problem often is there are not enough people to investigate the case.

Take fraud, whether it is an international fraud, an interstate fraud, or a fraud that is committed entirely on Wall Street. It is a very resource intensive investigation. You do not oftentimes need new laws to deal with those sorts of crimes. What you need are more agents, more accountants, more lawyers, more assets like that to look into the problem.

If you take the people that you need to investigate those crimes that only the Federal Government can handle away from that responsibility and give them the responsibility of handling things that the state and locals can handle, you are hurting the Nation's interest in law enforcement.

Mrs. DINGELL. Well, I want to ask Mr. Schoppmeyer a question because my concern is that state and local governments are already complaining about the lack of resources to do what they do, and I do believe it is critical that we keep our Federal lands safe. So where is this delicate balance?

Congress, I believe, has not done an adequate job of funding our land management agencies overall, and it has had an impact on law enforcement.

Mr. Schoppmeyer, would you describe some of the negative consequences of the budget cuts that we have seen over the years and perhaps give your observations as to what would happen if state and local were to have responsibility for Federal lands as well?

Mr. SCHOPPMEYER. Well, with all due respect to Mr. Larkin, I think some of the points that he is missing here are that the Lacey Act, we will take for instance, is the oldest conservation law in the United States. It goes back to 1900. Specifically the Lacey Act regulates the interstate or foreign commerce of illegally taken fish, wildlife, and plants. In such, as Mr. Larkin talks about, sophisticated complex civil and criminal cases involving the Lacey Act, the states are ill equipped to deal with it. The county is ill equipped to deal with it.

Quite honestly, if you did not have NOAA agents and Federal Fish and Wildlife agents enforcing the Lacey Act, it would not get done.

The other issue that came up with the FOCUS Act that was introduced by Senator Rand Paul is that, specifically, why don't we just create individual acts to protect rhinos and elephants. Well, you just cannot do that. I mean, it has to be wide-sweeping legislation.

You know, questions are asked, "Well, why do we enforce other country's laws?" Because they are even more ill equipped than we are to deal with these issues.

I personally would like to be able to know, even if I have never seen one in the wild, that a rhino exists and that an elephant exists. When it comes to the resources, the one thing that Mr. Larkin and I disagree on is you will never—and we represent the FBI, by the way; they have their own agents' association, but I am the Agency Affairs President—I can tell you that you will never see an FBI agent unless he is asked into an investigation, because there may be other things going on with terrorism funding and things like that, that are their other jurisdiction. You are not going to see an FBI agent out in the woods. It is just not going to happen.

Mrs. DINGELL. Well, let me ask you as our time is running out. Why is being a law enforcement officer for a land management agency different than other law enforcement jobs?

Mr. SCHOPPMEYER. We go through the same training at the Federal Law Enforcement Training Center, and then we branch off to go to our individual agencies for training. It is entirely different. It is called nontraditional law enforcement.

We protect natural resources. We also protect the public that visits these parks. Visitor safety protection is a high priority with the Forest Service, with the Park Service, and with Fish and Wildlife.

It really does come down to the fact that it is a specialized area, and you've got to want to be a natural resource law enforcement officer.

Mrs. DINGELL. I am out of time, Mr. Chairman.

Mr. GOHMERT. Thank you.

At this time I will recognize Mrs. Radewagen for 5 minutes.

Mrs. RADEWAGEN. Thank you, Mr. Chairman and Ranking Member.

Mr. Ehnes, one of our witnesses is very critical of the impact your hobby has on the environment. Is this the sort of hostility you face from Federal law enforcement, or would this be an example of a rare exception that poisons the well at a time when you are trying to build trust with the agencies?

Mr. EHNES. Mr. Chairman, Congresswoman, it is an attitude that does exist in some agencies, and we have done, I think, a very good job in many areas of building very strong relationships with the Forest Service.

The stove-piping is helping damage those recreations from the standpoint that we have good communications with the Forest supervisors, the district rangers, the recreation staff; and in my personal experience with the Lewis and Clark, I will call all of those people friends. We work very closely to make sure that our resource for our recreation is managed well and the people are educated.

In the example that I gave of the checkpoint that the LEO set up at one of our rides, it was perplexing to our riders because we as an organization feel as though we have a very strong relationship and did not understand why that had to happen that way. It would have been a great opportunity for the LEO to introduce himself to our riders and actually enhance the relationship had that person come into the camp.

If the communication or the direction from the Forest supervisor or the district ranger would have been in place, that's probably what would have happened because it would have heard about the strength of that relationship.

Mrs. RADEWAGEN. Thank you.

Sheriff Brown, as an elected sheriff, you have a fundamental level of accountability that your colleagues in the Forest Service do not. How does this undermine your ability to keep your constituents safe?

Sheriff BROWN. The difference is exactly that. Much like all of you are elected and you have a responsibility to the citizens that put you here in Washington, I have that same responsibility. When there are problems in my county, those phone calls come to my office.

I cannot deal with either disciplinary issues or officer conduct issues with the Forest Service LEO in my county. However, if we have a good relationship, and I will tell you that I do today; and I can tell you that 15 years ago I did not. Things have changed for me in my county, and I have the ability to work with the Special Agent and the ability to speak directly with the Director here in Washington.

If there are issues, we can talk those things through; and I have to be able to assure the people that elected me, that put me in the position that I am in, that those issues are being addressed. Much like I would hold my deputies accountable, I expect the Forest Service to hold their officers accountable as well.

Mrs. RADEWAGEN. Mr. Larkin, are there examples of decriminalizing regulatory offenses, or is this a genie out of the bottle situation where reversing course is near impossible?

Mr. LARKIN. I cannot think of any specific instances where Congress had decriminalized existing criminal programs in regulatory agencies, but it does mean that Congress should not consider this a worthwhile effort.

For example, it is often the case that Congress adds small-scale criminal provisions to different pieces of legislation, maybe making something a misdemeanor or a minor offense so they can then draw on the existing law enforcement agencies to do the work.

Over time then you will see that people will try to accumulate these crimes into larger crimes and felonies and add to the authority of agencies by creating some new programs.

In my view what Congress should do is reconsider the entire allocation of Federal criminal investigation responsibilities and transfer the authority that regulatory agencies' criminal programs currently have, transfer these to the FBI.

Mrs. RADEWAGEN. Thank you, Mr. Chairman. I yield back.

Mr. GOHMERT. Thank you very much.

At this time the Chair recognizes Mr. Gallego for 5 minutes.

Mr. GALLEGO. Thank you, Mr. Chairman.

Mr. Schoppmeyer, I apologize. Did I say that correctly?

Mr. SCHOPPMEYER. Yes.

Mr. GALLEGO. What is the feeling among some of our agents, at least how they are feeling especially with the kind of rhetoric that Cliven Bundy is putting out there—not the racist rhetoric but the anti-government, anti-environmental rhetoric that basically I believe puts a lot of our men and women in a very weird and awkward position when trying to enforce what we understand are our grazing laws?

Mr. SCHOPPMEYER. Well, I can say this. With regards to the Cliven Bundy situation, our agents and officers that were involved in that situation, BLM and the other agencies, they are concerned. They are concerned about personal safety, they are concerned for their families; and that is not an understatement.

As far as the relationship goes, I find it so bizarre that we can have local and county law enforcement be at odds with Federal law enforcement in the Cliven Bundy situation during that incident; yet several months later during Police Week here, right here in Washington, DC, that we can have those officers standing shoulder to shoulder to respect those that have fallen. It is bizarre to me that that situation can occur.

Again, with respect to your question, I think there is great concern by all of the land management agencies.

Mr. GALLEGO. Thank you.

This question is for Mr. Larkin and Mr. Schoppmeyer.

I am glad that we are starting to focus on just the law enforcement questions regarding the agency, but I also agree that there are overall serious questions that must be answered. We are dealing with human lives as well as, I guess, animal lives too. But one of the things I think we are missing, is instead of talking about removing criminal penalties from a very effective conservation law and taking away firearms of those tasked to enforce the law, I want to talk about some of the weapons that are coming down.

More specifically, I want to talk about the 1033 Program that brings surplus heavy weaponry onto local and state law enforcements, as well as Federal land management agencies. Right now about 8,000 agencies currently get material through the 1033 Program from the Department of Defense, including the National Park Service. The program was brought to wide attention by the shooting of Michael Brown in Ferguson.

Since then, we have learned that the 1033 gear has been given to schools and colleges. We have also learned that some local law enforcement wants to return the equipment, but the Department of Defense will not take it back.

The program was originally intended to focus the materials on counter-narcotics operations, and it is not working. There is enough common ground that I think in this committee that we can dig into the over-militarization question in a very bipartisan way, and I hope we do, and I hope it does.

Mr. Larkin, you have written a lot about over-criminalization. Do you think the 1033 Program is only a problem for land management agencies, or are there problems with the program beyond that, and the whole concept of it?

Mr. LARKIN. The latter.

Mr. GALLEGO. Say again. I am sorry.

Mr. LARKIN. The latter.

Mr. GALLEGO. The latter. Thank you.

Mr. LARKIN. I think what you have is an unfortunate circumstance where we have had an over-proliferation of SWAT teams and military equipment used by law enforcement departments. There are not nearly the number of instances where that is necessary.

The problem is, once you start creating SWAT teams, everybody wants one. You could call it the curse of testosterone, if you will. You have this problem not only by giving this authority to Federal regulatory agencies, but by giving military equipment to too many state and local agencies.

The proliferation or over-militarization of law enforcement is only going to endanger the relationships that law enforcement needs with the public.

I was a Federal agent. I worked in the EPA criminal program. I could not have gotten my job done without the work of state and local law enforcement. If law enforcement damages that relationship, and if both of them damage the relationship with the public, no one is going to benefit.

Mr. GALLEGO. Thank you.

Mr. Schoppmeyer, the same question to you.

Mr. SCHOPPMEYER. Yes, I would say that it is on a case-by-case basis with the natural resource agencies. We know that there is DTO activity up as far as the Upper Peninsula of Michigan; and quite honestly, your only enforcement up there besides Border Patrol and Customs and Border Protection is your land management agencies.

I, as an agent or officer, would not want to confront somebody from the Mexican cartel or something with just a standard firearm that is issued to me as a sidearm.

Then there is the whole issue of the visiting public up in that area who quite honestly could run into a very dangerous situation.

So I think it is a case-by-case basis.

Mr. GALLEGO. Thank you.

I yield back my time.

Mr. GOHMERT. Thank you.

Along those lines, we received a letter from the American Civil Liberties Union; and, after consulting with the Ranking Member, I ask unanimous consent that this letter be added for the record. It is interesting when The Heritage and ACLU agree on a subject like this.

[The letter from the American Civil Liberties Union offered by Mr. Gohmert follows:]

ACLU—AMERICAN CIVIL LIBERTIES UNION,
WASHINGTON, DC,
JULY 28, 2015.

Hon. LOUIE GOHMERT, *Chairman*,
House Subcommittee on Oversight and Investigations,
Committee on Natural Resources,
1324 Longworth House Office Building,
Washington, DC 20515.

Hon. DEBBIE DINGELL, *Ranking Member*,
House Subcommittee on Oversight and Investigations,
Committee on Natural Resources,
1324 Longworth House Office Building,
Washington, DC 20515.

Re: ACLU Requests Examination of Interior's Acquisition of Military Weapons and Equipment

DEAR CHAIRMAN GOHMERT AND RANKING MEMBER DINGELL:

The American Civil Liberties Union (ACLU) commends the Oversight and Investigations Subcommittee of the U.S. House Natural Resources Committee for holding a hearing on "Accountability, Policies, and Tactics of Law Enforcement within the Department of the Interior (DOI) and the U.S. Forest Service." We ask that the Committee examine the relationship between DOI and the Department of Defense (DOD) 1033 program, which provides military weapons and equipment to federal, state, and local law enforcement agencies. We have concerns with the militarization of DOI bureaus like the National Park Service (NPS), which has acquired 4,100 pieces of military equipment worth approximately $6 million over the past 25 years.[1]

The ACLU believes that the line between military and law enforcement cannot be blurred. Our opposition to militarization is consistent with the ACLU's nearly 100 year old mission to defend and preserve the individual rights and liberties that the Constitution and the laws of the United States guarantee everyone in this country. As the nation's guardian of liberty, and with more than a million members, activists, and supporters nationwide, the ACLU advances the principle that every individual's rights must be protected equally under the law, regardless of race, religion, gender, sexual orientation, disability, or national origin.

The DOD 1033 Program is authorized by Section 1033 of the National Defense Authorization Act of 1997. It permits the Secretary of Defense to transfer, without charge, excess DOD supplies and equipment to federal, state, and local law enforcement agencies.[2] Since the 1990s, the Defense Logistics Agency has transferred excess military equipment to approximately 8,000 federal and state law enforcement agencies and has provided $5.1 B in total property.[3] This equipment includes but is not limited to, military-grade vehicles, grenades, assault rifles, and night vision equipment.

We have concerns that this program has led to militarized policing, which we raise in our recent report, *War Comes Home: The Excessive Militarization of American Policing*[4]. As the nation watched Ferguson Missouri, in the aftermath of the death of Michael Brown, it saw a dangerously militarized response by law enforcement. However, militarized policing is not limited to state and local law enforcement. For example, in 2010, a multi-agency taskforce, including armed officers from the Food and Drug Agency, raided a Venice, California organic grocery store suspected of using raw milk.[5] The following year, armed federal agents with the Department of Education's OIG smashed down the door of a Stockton, California home and handcuffed a man suspected of student financial aid fraud.[6]

We are concerned by the relationship between the DOD 1033 program and some of the Department of Interior agencies. While the National Park Service handbook explicitly limits the agency's ability to acquire firearms "to the minimum needed for an effective law enforcement program," the service has obtained thousands of handguns, high-powered assault rifles, bayonets, and shotguns through this program. And unfortunately, an exact accounting of these thousands of weapons is not known as a 2013 Inspector General report identified a poorly managed inventory.[7]

We fear that the acquisition of military weapons and equipment increases the potential for excessive policing, such as the 2013 raid of a small mining operation in Chicken, Alaska. During this raid, a heavily armed and armored multi-agency taskforce, including officers from the National Park Service and Fish and Wildlife Service, descended upon several mines to search for Clean Water Act violations.[8] Alaska Governor Sean Parnell voiced his deep concern, noting that the use of armed and body-armor-wearing officers who were relatively unfamiliar with the area put

---

[1] Matthew Renda, *Does Yosemite Really Need $435,000 of Military Equipment?*, The Edge, January 7, 2014.

[2] The White House, *Review: Federal Support for Local Law Enforcement Equipment Acquisition*, December 2014, *available at* https://www.whitehouse.gov/sites/default/files/docs/federal_support_for_local_law_enforcement_equipment_acquisition.pdf.

[3] Id.

[4] See ACLU, *War Comes Home: The Excessive Militarization of American Policing*, June 23, 2014, *available at* https://www.aclu.org/sites/default/files/assets/jus14-warcomeshome-report-web-re11.pdf.

[5] P.J. Huffstutter, *Raw-food raid Highlights a Hunger*, The Los Angeles Times, July 25, 2010.

[6] Elizabeth Flock, *Education Department Agents Raids California Home*, The Washington Post, June 8, 2011.

[7] Supra note 1.

[8] Valerie Richardson, *EPA Facing Fire for Armed Raid on Mine in Chicken, Alaska: Population 7*. Washington Times, October 11, 2013.

people at risk.[9] We worry that these events will only become more frequent and dangerous with the continued acquisition of military equipment by law enforcement at all levels.

The ACLU understands the desire to ensure the safety of both federal employees and civilians but we question the necessity of military-grade equipment in achieving that end. Through greater transparency, more oversight, policies that encourage restraint, and limitations on federal incentives, we can foster a law enforcement culture that honors its mission to protect and serve.

We appreciate the Subcommittee's commitment to ensuring accountability in law enforcement as demonstrated by the call for a hearing and respectfully request an examination of the relationship between DOD 1033 and the Department of the Interior. If you have any questions, please feel free to contact Kanya Bennett, Legislative Counsel.

Sincerely,

MICHAEL W. MACLEOD-BALL,
Acting Director.

KANYA BENNETT,
Legislative Counsel.

————

Mr. GOHMERT. At this time the Chair recognizes Mr. Mooney for 5 minutes.

Mr. MOONEY. Thank you, Mr. Chairman.

Mr. Ehnes, in your testimony you singled out an experience where law enforcement set up a check station. Can you elaborate on what created an issue there and possibly damaged trust with the Forest Service?

Mr. EHNES. Mr. Congressman, yes; and I want to be clear that check stations are an important tool in the right areas. I live in Montana and have recreated there for 45 years on public land, and I nor anybody that I am acquainted with has ever encountered a check station on a trail anywhere. So, it is not a tool that gets applied in Montana on a consistent basis.

There are places where it is appropriate. In this situation, the permitted event was with the Great Falls Trail Bike Riders and Montana Trail Vehicle Riders. As I mentioned, we go through a great deal of effort to make sure that compliance is perfect, that our people are examples, and that we use those events to educate anybody that we run into.

I think that had we had the opportunity for enforcement to be informed about our relationship with the Forest and have them engaged with us at the trail head, it could have been an opportunity for us to build a strong relationship. We really want to work with enforcement to help them do a better job, understand how to report crimes, all of those things that could have resulted in a better outcome.

The fact that they were out just a little ways from the trail head with clearly the intent of checking our members who are the shining stars, if you will, of the OHV community, did damage their trust because they felt a little bit ambushed.

Mr. MOONEY. Thank you for expanding on that.

Sheriff Brown, a question for you. I have one of the U.S. Fish and Wildlife Service Training Centers in my district, actually in

[9] Sean Doogan, *Probe Into Raid of Chicken Miners by Gun-toting EPA Investigators Finds No Laws Broken.* Alaska Dispatch News, March 13, 2014.

the county I live in, and I have toured it. They are good people; but I also understand you've got to have as clear as possible lines of delineation of whose job is what, who enforces what, where your demarcations are.

In your opinion, what do you view as the proper role of Forest Service law enforcement officers?

Sheriff BROWN. Well, I think everything that they do that is consistent with their mission. There is no imaginary line where the national forest starts and the county ends. The county's boundaries surround the national forest. The sheriff has complete authority and jurisdiction on all state laws within that national forest.

We typically will not enforce Code of Federal Regulation; Forest Service will do that. It typically and traditionally was timber theft, resource protection issues, especially when there was a great deal of logging occurring, which there is not today. So, one might argue there is not a great deal of timber theft, but there are a lot of resource issues.

In addition to that, I think sheriffs across the West concur that these armed officers—and by no means are we suggesting we disarm the Forest Service—but these armed officers have responsibility if they are going to be out there to make sure that if something is happening that is a detriment to a forest user or forest visitor, that they are authorized and trained to take action.

But, we also want recognition of the sovereignty of the Office of Sheriff, and we want the Forest Service to recognize and work with sheriffs and communicate with sheriffs. I think that the suggestion of the local oversight, the law enforcement councils for local oversight are going to give us that opportunity to work together and communicate very specifically on issues that have come out of Montana on this trail ride.

If law enforcement is communicating with the users of the forest, with the sheriff in that county, we are going to have a much, much better working relationship.

Mr. MOONEY. And we have a minute left on my time, Sheriff, but a follow-up.

In addition to understanding the proper roles, accountability would also be important. It appears sometimes issues between law enforcement agencies can boil down to personalities, but they fester on because of lack of accountability from various Federal agencies.

So in your view, what are the options available to increase accountability?

Sheriff BROWN. Two things. The local councils are the first thing. If the Special Agent in Charge in my particular case has Oregon, Washington, and Alaska. If we are regularly meeting, and through the Western States Sheriffs' Association we created a Memorandum of Agreement, the Forest Service has signed onto it, and it calls for that accountability issue.

When a sheriff can make a complaint to a captain or a SAC, and that SAC or captain comes back and says, "Sheriff, here is how we have addressed it. Here is the resolution." We then can go back to our constituent and say, "Listen. It is taken care of. I can assure you of that."

Those are the kinds of things I think through local oversight that we will be able to resolve much quicker than we have in the past.

Mr. MOONEY. Thank you.

I yield back my second.

Mr. GOHMERT. I thank the gentleman.

At this time the Chair recognizes the gentleman from Arkansas, Mr. Westerman, for 5 minutes.

Mr. WESTERMAN. Thank you, Mr. Chairman, and thank you for coming here today for this important hearing.

I will add that I have a lot of national forests in my district, and I spend a lot of time driving through them. Last year on the campaign trail, there was a one-vehicle accident in a very remote area; and Forest Service law enforcement were the first ones on the scene. They were the first responders. It was in an area where there was no cell phone reception, but they were able to use their radios and get other emergency personnel there.

So, they often work in remote areas by themselves, and I think the folks on the ground are doing a fantastic job at least in the national forest where I live.

Mr. Larkin, in his testimony Mr. Schoppmeyer explained that decriminalizing the Lacey Act would cripple the good guys in the fight to keep visitors safe and our greatest national treasures accessible to all. Could you give us your perspective on this view?

Mr. LARKIN. I think he is wrong for several reasons. In the first place, the Lacey Act is unconstitutional. As I explained in my written statement, the Lacey Act delegates authority to foreign officials, officials of foreign governments, to define elements of crimes that can be prosecuted in the U.S. courts. That violates Articles I and II of the Constitution, as well as the due process clause.

Second, the U.S. Marshal Service or the FBI also have authority in the areas that now the Fish and Wildlife Service works. I believe that it would be better to transfer the authority that we have now given to different agencies, such as the Fish and Wildlife Service, to the U.S. Marshal Service or the FBI, so that you can take advantage not simply of economies of scale, but of the greater long-term experience and greater access to SWAT units and the like when it is necessary in order to enforce the laws that are necessary in those areas.

Third, state and local law enforcement officers can be made Special Deputy U.S. Marshals in areas that are subject to either exclusive or concurrent Federal jurisdiction, and so state and local law enforcement officers can be used to deal with those sorts of crimes.

Fourth, the Lacey Act is a very specialized statute. The Federal Assimilative Crimes Act incorporates, for any particular area that is within Federal jurisdiction, state and local offenses. So Federal law enforcement officers can enforce those state and local offenses even if there is not a similar Federal crime on the books.

So, eliminating the Lacey Act will in no way endanger the lives or safety of the people who benefit from using our national parks.

Mr. WESTERMAN. Thank you.

Sheriff Brown, I appreciate your suggestions to improve law enforcement with the Forest Service. Some would suggest that they are merely a paranoid attempt to reduce the authority of the Federal Government. Without legitimizing that opinion, can you speak to why this is a question of safety and not just political theater?

Sheriff BROWN. The issue really stems, I guess, or goes back to the basic understanding of our community—what does the sheriff do and what does the Forest Service do? When it comes to safety, the calls that I am getting, the calls that I have received have been, "Sheriff, I got stopped," or, "I was stopped," or, "I was contacted by a Forest Service guy wearing a gun. Does he have jurisdiction? Does she have jurisdiction?" It is that confusion in some of the minds of the people that have had to deal with that.

Then an explanation, I think, that is warranted that says, "OK. Let me try and explain to you. Here is what they can do. Here is how they enforce it under Code of Federal Regulation, and here is where their authority starts or stops."

Well, if that continued contact, in my particular case, rises to a point where somebody feels they are being harassed or constantly picked on, et cetera, and I cannot get resolution through the local patrol captain or the local SAC, which for a lot of years we could not, then I think it creates a safety issue.

Until we open up those lines of communication and we get an understanding from all sides that are involved in this, we will not resolve these issues. Things are better today than they have been in the last 5, 6, 7 years, and I think it is directly tied to the relationship that the Western State Sheriffs has developed with the Director of Law Enforcement for the Forest Service.

We have a new Director at the BLM. We are working on that relationship as well. Ninety percent of the public lands in this country are out West. I think things for the most part are good, but there are places where we have to work on relationships, communication, and an understanding of authority.

Mr. WESTERMAN. Thank you, Mr. Chairman.

Mr. GOHMERT. Thank you.

At this time, I will recognize the Chairman of the Full Committee, the distinguished Chairman Bishop, for 5 minutes.

Mr. BISHOP. Thank you. Louie, I appreciate that.

Sheriff Brown, let me ask you a couple of questions if I could, because I think this is a significant issue; and I appreciate all four of you for being here talking about it. I think we need to go into greater detail on this particular issue at the same time.

You talked about how your situation is better than it was 15 years ago. Is that due to the personalities involved or is there a structural reason for that?

Sheriff BROWN. It is not structural because the Forest Service structure for their command has not changed in 15 years. It is people.

Mr. BISHOP. So it is the personalities?

Sheriff BROWN. In my case, it is a person. There was no accountability for that person in my county. That person has since retired, and things began to get a little bit better.

Mr. BISHOP. It would be nice if we can guarantee that and not just rely on the personalities of individuals involved, recognizing that if you have the right people almost anything can be done. If you do not, everything screws up somehow.

Sheriff BROWN. That is right.

Mr. BISHOP. So, Sheriff, I understand that each Forest Service, BLM, and other Federal law enforcement agencies have to go through several months of training at a training center, different ones. Are you aware of any training modules that teach interaction with local law enforcement in these training centers?

Sheriff BROWN. That is a great question. I am not, and in fact, that is something the Western Sheriffs have begun talking about, and especially with a service provider that may be able to assist us in establishing either on-line or in-person training courses that will talk about that very thing, that interaction, that scope of authority, the jurisdiction, how we intermingle within our public lands, within our counties.

Mr. BISHOP. So obviously, if we do not have those modules going, the sheriffs' organizations have not had any input into that. That would be something structurally that we could do to improve the situation.

What would your view be of having a national law enforcement review board for each agency that would include not only the Federal line officers, but the county sheriffs that could review specific concerns and policy changes?

Sheriff BROWN. My first thought about that is one more layer of bureaucracy is going to muddy the water even more than it may already be. I think the best chance for oversight comes at the local level; and I think establishing these law enforcement councils at the local level where the sheriff, Special Agent from the BLM, Special Agent from the Forest Service, the patrol captains and commanders from both of those public agencies are involved are going to be our best opportunity for oversight.

Mr. BISHOP. OK. If I ask you probably the most important reason why we "de-stovepipe" these organizations, if we could do that— that is not a word, but it is the best I could come up with—"de-stovepipe" these organizations if they would provide better coordination with county sheriffs and serve the public?

Sheriff BROWN. My answer to that is back when the Forest Service was, I guess, a strong agency both financially and people-wise—the district rangers, the Forest supervisors, the regional foresters, those people lived in our communities; their kids went to school with our kids; they went to the same churches together. We knew each other, we worked with each other, and who best knows what needs to happen on the national forest or that particular ranger district than a district ranger or a Forest supervisor?

Those people used to be within the line of authority of the law enforcement component as well. When the structure changed, that changed, and our relationships began to change. We no longer negotiate co-op agreements with our district ranger. We no longer sit and talk about operational planning for law enforcement or functions on the national forest with our Forest supervisor or our district ranger. They are not in that chain of command anymore.

I know there are particular reasons why maybe "de-stovepiping," if you will, will not work; but I think that there has to be a re-integration somehow at the local level of the law enforcement.

Mr. BISHOP. We need to try that. I realize we have had a lot of conversation about Forest Service, but BLM has the same situation. In my state, it is even more significant; and once again, dealing with personality, I would like to have some kind of structural concept in there that could minimize those personality conflicts when they do exist, or at least resolve them much quicker than they have—even to the example when we had some hearings a couple of years ago on Park Service law enforcement, to realize you have a couple of different entities, one law enforcement, that only actually the Park Service does not even have any control over; they are all on their own that deal with only three sections of this country.

All those issues need to be resolved in some particular way, so I am glad we are starting this process of trying to find out some ways that we can solve these issues without relying on simply the right people having the right personalities at the right time.

Thank you, Mr. Chairman.

Mr. GOHMERT. I thank the Chairman.

I recognize myself for 5 minutes.

Following that up, it does seem rather ridiculous that there would be any area in the country where a resolution of conflict would be resolved after many years or even decades of service by one individual, that he finally retires and that makes things better.

I know Mr. Schoppmeyer mentioned that you do not find FBI in the woods. But in east Texas, in my own personal experience—having been a prosecutor, a judge, and a chief justice, I have seen and read lots of testimony; I have talked to law enforcement officers. We often have FBI in the woods because, Sheriff, they do exactly what you are talking about you would like to see between locals and Federal officers, and that is they meet together and they talk, and when there is a problem, they get together and they coordinate.

But here again, that also, as you being law enforcement would know, takes sometimes a trust. With the FBI, that suffered back during the Bush administration under Director Mueller, who back then had a 5-year "up or out" policy. We would get somebody good, the local law enforcement would start to trust him, and then they would be up or out.

I complained bitterly about that policy. It has changed now, but, Sheriff, do you have any formal proposal as to how that structure might be set up between local and Federal officials to coordinate better?

Sheriff BROWN. There are models across, I am sure, many states. In my particular region, we have two law enforcement councils that the membership is made up of all of the local police departments and the county sheriffs within a three- to four-county region. And those issues are really to talk about common problems.

In one particular county, it is a county with nine different police departments with one prosecuting attorney. That particular prosecuting attorney is dealing with various issues, whether it is tied to pursuits, or drug cases, or child sex abuse cases; so there is some uniformity in discussions at these local law enforcement councils.

I am suggesting we can accomplish much the same thing if we are meeting with our Federal land manager or law enforcement agencies to talk about operational planning—whether the Rainbow Festival is coming to your county next year, or whether it is off-road vehicle use, or trail use, or trail construction, that's happening a lot in my county that is illegal.

But those things, I think, have to be talked about. I do not want to do the job of a Federal law enforcement officer. I do not want to do resource protection issues. By default, we do some of that under state law, but I do not have either the resources or the time to do that.

But if they are going to be out there doing it, there are going to be times when they are coming across things that are primarily and traditionally the role of the sheriff, and we need to de-conflict those.

Mr. GOHMERT. Sheriff, my time is running out, but let me direct you specifically to the Gibson guitar case, where as I understand, that was a Lacey Act enforcement; and you have Federal law enforcement come busting in, armed to the teeth, and people are just making guitars.

If, in a situation like that, you were notified that in your county somebody was manufacturing guitars and there was concern that they were using wood that was not properly imported, would you be willing to send a deputy along with people in suits and no weapons as they went in and asked for records from the guitar maker?

Sheriff BROWN. Not only would I be willing, but I would demand it in my county.

Mr. GOHMERT. So, that can be done without arming the Federal people to the teeth, correct?

Sheriff BROWN. Yes, sir.

Mr. GOHMERT. I agreed with so much in the letter from the ACLU and so much that conforms to what, Mr. Larkin, you have said with one exception. I have seen the difference that it can make when local law enforcement, and I would also presume with Federal officials, if they have defensive equipment from the military, say, bulletproof vests.

Would you have a problem with defensive equipment being provided?

Mr. LARKIN. Not at all. That is entirely appropriate.

Mr. GOHMERT. All right. Thank you.

My time has expired. Let me consult with the Ranking Member.

I recognize the Ranking Member for a unanimous consent.

Mrs. DINGELL. I would ask unanimous consent to enter into the record the testimony of Marcus Asner to the Fishery Subcommittee in 2013 on why Americans should have to comply with foreign law.

Mr. Asner testified that other U.S. laws reference foreign laws and clarified that the Lacey Act does not penalize those that violate foreign law nor implement it.

As to earlier comments about the Lacey Act, which was passed in 1900, being unconstitutional, the Supreme Court has not directly addressed it or taken up any challenges. Every circuit court that has been asked to consider the issue has upheld the Lacey Act against constitutional challenges.

The argument that the Lacey Act's reliance on foreign laws is unconstitutional has been described as patently frivolous, without merit, and neither original nor meritorious by courts that it has been brought up in.

Mr. GOHMERT. So the request was for the testimony?

Mrs. DINGELL. To enter this testimony into the record.

Mr. GOHMERT. Without objection, so ordered.

Mrs. DINGELL. Thank you.

Mr. GOHMERT. And the ACLU letter, without objection, is entered as part of the record.

Hearing nothing further at this time, we appreciate all of your testimony. We appreciate your time here. If you have anything additionally you would like to have entered into the record, then please submit that. The record will be open for 10 business days for these responses, and that is under Committee Rule 4(h).

If there is nothing further in the way of further business, without objection, the committee stands adjourned. Thank you.

[Whereupon, at 11:49 a.m., the subcommittee was adjourned.]

[LIST OF DOCUMENTS SUBMITTED FOR THE RECORD RETAINED IN THE COMMITTEE'S OFFICIAL FILES]

—Letter dated January 30, 2014 from Congressman Mark Meadows to Phyllis Fong, Inspector General at the Department of Agriculture, and Mary Kendall, Deputy Inspector General with the Office of the Inspector General at the Department of the Interior regarding the legality of law enforcement actions taken by the U.S. Fish and Wildlife Service and U.S. Forest Service during "Operation Something Bruin."

—Response Letter dated March 25, 2014 from Mary Kendall, Deputy Inspector General with the Office of the Inspector General at the Department of the Interior, to Congressman Mark Meadows regarding his inquiry on the legality of law enforcement actions taken by the U.S. Fish and Wildlife Service and U.S. Forest Service during "Operation Something Bruin."

—Response Letter dated March 26, 2014 from Phyllis Fong, Inspector General at the Department of Agriculture, to Congressman Mark Meadows regarding his inquiry on the legality of law enforcement actions taken by the U.S. Fish and Wildlife Service and U.S. Forest Service during "Operation Something Bruin."

—Letter dated August 4, 2015 from the North American Wildlife Enforcement Officers Association to Chairman Gohmert and Ranking Member Dingell in regards to the Oversight hearing dated July 28, 2015.

—Testimony of Marcus Asner before the Committee on Natural Resources, Subcommittee on Fisheries, Wildlife, Oceans and Insular Affairs for hearing titled, "Why Should Americans Have to Comply with the Laws of Foreign Nations?," dated July 17, 2013.

○

www.ingramcontent.com/pod-product-compliance
Lightning Source LLC
Chambersburg PA
CBHW081749280526
45789CB00008B/2791